30-minute indian

30-minute indian

Sunil Vijayakar

Photography by William Reavell

hamlyn

A Pyramid Paperback from Hamlyn

First published in Great Britain in 2000 by Hamlyn,
a division of Octopus Publishing Group Ltd
2–4 Heron Quays, London E14 4JP

This revised edition published 2004

ISBN-13: 978-0-600-61026-7
ISBN-10: 0-600-61026-8

A CIP catalogue record for this book is available
from the British Library

Printed and bound in China

10 9 8 7 6 5 4 3 2

NOTES

1 The Department of Health advises that eggs
should not be consumed raw. It is prudent for
more vulnerable people such as pregnant and
nursing mothers, invalids, the elderly, babies and
young children to avoid uncooked or lightly cooked
dishes made with eggs.

2 Meat and poultry should be cooked thoroughly.
To test if poultry is cooked, pierce the flesh
through the thickest part with a skewer or fork –
the juices should run clear, never pink or red.

3 This book includes dishes made with nuts and
nut derivatives. It is advisable for those with
known allergic reactions to nuts and nut
derivatives and those who may be potentially
vulnerable to these allergies, such as pregnant and
nursing mothers, invalids, the elderly, babies and
children, to avoid dishes made with nuts and nut
oils. It is also prudent to check the labels of pre-
prepared ingredients for the possible inclusion of
nut derivatives.

contents

introduction

I think my love of food stems from the Sunday mornings I spent with my father as a young boy, growing up in Bombay. A film director with a hectic work and social life, he would make Sunday the day when he would stop and cook a big lunch for a large group of family and friends. He would pile me into his Morris Minor and off we would head for the bustling bazaars and markets. Armed with shopping bags, we would wander through endless aisles of vegetable and fruit stalls, then into open courtyards full of fresh fish and shellfish, piled on to blocks of ice, and into tiny little stalls with colourful pyramids of spices, nuts and dried fruits.

This was an experience that assailed all the senses; the visual feast of wicker baskets piled high with bright green bunches of fresh coriander, mint and fenugreek. Wooden crates of mangoes, papayas and ruby-red pomegranates; mountains of fresh ginger, onions and garlic. The tactile experience of touching and tasting the produce, the aromas of all the dried spices and, above all, the cacophony of the market sellers plying their wares. Laden with our shopping, we would wend our way home and into the kitchen, where dad would effortlessly conjure up a veritable feast, all the time talking with great

passion about different foods and ingredients and making me his official taster. He instilled in me a love and passion for food, with his relaxed attitude to preparation and cooking, and most importantly the gift and joy of sharing food.

In this book and through these recipes, I hope I can share with you some of the dishes I have enjoyed and continue to enjoy cooking on a frequent basis. The frenetic pace of our modern life often limits the time we have to spend preparing, cooking and experimenting with food. These recipes are all quick and easy to prepare and will give you a taste of Indian cuisine, which you can easily incorporate into your cooking on a daily basis.

A well-stocked storecupboard of basic ingredients and spices is essential. Most of these can be bought in large supermarkets, but I would urge you to go to an Indian or Asian greengrocer and stock up. All spices, whole or ground, should be stored in airtight containers in a cool, dark place. Some of the recipes call for a long list of spices and other ingredients. Do not let this intimidate you; just make sure that you have everything at hand before you start to cook and the rest will be easy. You will realize that cooking Indian food is like painting a picture; if you have an organized palette to work with, you can create anything you desire.

The main ingredients for cooking wonderful food are not, however, to be found in jars, bazaars or supermarkets, but in the love and joy of cooking, eating and sharing food.

glossary

amchur Raw, green mango powder, pale yellow in colour. Used in dishes to add tartness with a hint of sweetness. If unavailable, substitute ½ teaspoon of lemon or lime juice for 1 teaspoon of amchur.

asafoetida A resin from the plant, it is extremely strong in flavour and aroma and is used only in tiny quantities. It is available in small, plastic boxes and should be stored tightly closed. As well as flavour, asafoetida has great digestive powers.

atta or chapatti flour This medium-grade flour is used to make most Indian unleavened breads. This may be bought at any Indian grocers. Ordinary wholemeal flour may also be used for Indian breads, very well sieved.

basmati rice This distinctive long-grain rice is very popular as an accompaniment to meat and vegetable dishes.

cardamom Little green pods with tiny black-brown seeds, very aromatic in flavour. They come in three varieties: green, white and black. The green and white pods can be used for both sweet and savoury dishes or to flavour rice, the black only for savoury dishes. The pods are used whole in rice dishes or the seeds are lightly crushed or ground and used to flavour sweets and other dishes. It is one of the main components of garam masala.

cashew nuts Grown on the western coast of India, these nuts are used in curries, rice dishes and desserts. They are usually roasted or fried before being used.

cassia Also known as 'Chinese cinnamon', this bark is stronger in flavour than cinnamon and has a slightly thicker texture. It can easily be substituted with cinnamon, if unavailable.

chillies
dried These red chillies are used to flavour dishes, usually by frying them in hot oil. There are a few specific varieties used in Indian cooking such as the Kashmiri and Round chillies. Chilli flakes are also used to give a fiery 'heat' to food. Use with caution.
fresh green and red The chillies used in Indian food are usually the long, green, slender variety and can be very hot in flavour. To lessen the heat of a chilli when using, carefully remove the seeds by splitting the chilli in half lengthways, wearing gloves if need be. Fresh red chillies are simply ripened green chillies and have the same intensity of heat.
powder Mild, medium and hot chilli powders are made from ground dried chillies. If using for the first time, experiment with the amount that you use.

cinnamon Cinnamon is the thinly rolled inner bark of an evergreen tree that grows mainly in southern India and Sri Lanka, in Madagascar and in the West Indies. Used in stick or ground form, this bark is used to flavour rice dishes, curries and sweets. It can be substituted with cassia if the recipe calls for it.

cloves This very strongly-flavoured and aromatic spice is used in many curry and rice dishes. Ground cloves are used in very small quantities because of their pungency. It is also sometimes used to seal a betel leaf for serving after an Indian meal.

coconut
Fresh coconut flesh is widely used in many Indian dishes, grated or ground to a paste. To obtain the flesh from a coconut, the easiest way I have found is to put it into a thick polythene bag and slam it hard on a concrete floor. There will be some water in it, which you can save, and then you should prise the flesh from the tough outer shell with a sharp knife. Once this is done, remove the thin, brown skin using a vegetable peeler. To prepare grated coconut for a recipe, cut the flesh into small pieces and process in a food processor until you get tiny flakes. You can also use a conventional grater, which is time consuming but you will obtain a smoother texture. Grated coconut freezes well if stored in an airtight freezer bag and is always useful to have in store.

coconut milk
Providing texture and flavour for meat and vegetable dishes, this milk is widely available in supermarkets and is sold in 400 g (13 oz) cans.

coriander
dried This spice is sold as whole seeds, which are light brown and round, or as a ground powder. It is an essential spice in Indian cooking.
fresh This fragrant and aromatic herb is widely used in Indian cuisine and is an important ingredient for many dishes, chutneys and salads.

cumin
These brown, grain-like seeds are used whole, fried or roasted. In its ground form, cumin is an essential base to many Indian dishes, from curries to rice.

curry leaves
These leaves are small and dark green and are often sold fresh in Indian greengrocers. They are usually fried before use, to impart an aromatic flavour to any dish or pickle.

dhal
These are lentils and other pulses; there are over 60 different types. The better known are listed below, and are available in Indian grocery stores and large supermarkets.
masoor dhal are split, skinless, red lentils. They are dark brown when whole, but when split and the skin is removed, the colour is bright pinky orange.
moong dhal are split, skinless, moong lentils. They are dark green when whole, but once split and skinned, they are yellow and oval shaped.
channa dhal are split, black, gram lentils. They are from the chickpea family but are smaller and have a dark brown husk. When split and skinned, they are bright yellow and resemble yellow split peas. Gram flour (besan) is made from these lentils.

dhana-jeera
This is a mixture of ground coriander and cumin seeds, available from Asian greengrocers. You can make your own spice mix by grinding together 1 teaspoon of cumin seeds and 2 teaspoons of coriander seeds.

fennel seeds
These light green seeds have a flavour of aniseed and are slightly bigger than cumin seeds. They are also eaten, lightly roasted, after an Indian meal as a digestive.

fenugreek seeds and leaves
These tiny, pebble-like, mustard-yellow seeds have an earthy flavour and are mainly used in pickles and vegetarian cooking. When the seeds are sprouted, it results in a spinach-like leaf which is used to flavour breads and other dishes.

garam masala
This is a ground spice mix. It can be bought ready-made in commercial jars or packets. However, there is nothing like making your own, as it will have much more pungency and flavour. The main ingredients are cardamom, cinnamon or cassia, cloves and black peppercorns. Here is a recipe for making your own garam masala. Once made, store in an airtight jar and use when required.

1 tablespoon broken-up cassia or cinnamon sticks
1 tablespoon cardamom pods
1 teaspoon whole cloves
3 teaspoons cumin seeds
2 teaspoons black peppercorns

In a dry, hot frying pan, roast the spices for 1–2 mins or until you can smell the aroma. Leave to cool, then place in a coffee grinder and grind until you have a fine powder. Store in an airtight jar. This mixture will keep for up to 3–4 months.

garlic
Indispensable to most Indian cooking, fresh garlic is used peeled and finely crushed, chopped or sliced. A quick way to prepare crushed garlic is to use a fine grater.

ginger
This rhizome is an integral part of most Indian cooking, along with garlic and onions (the essential base of most Indian food). Make sure you get fresh ginger which has a smooth, light brown skin. To use, peel and either slice into slivers or fine dice, or finely grate, saving and using any juice.

gram flour (besan)
A fine, pale yellow-coloured flour made from chickpeas. It is used in many recipes, from breads to vegetable curries.

green mangoes
The unripe fruit with green skin is used mainly as a pickle ingredient and sometimes to add a tangy flavour to curries.

jaggery
Raw cane sugar, sold in blocks or moulds and widely used to sweeten or balance any hot, spicy dish. However, if not available, soft brown cane sugar can easily replace it.

mango pulp
A versatile ingredient, usually used to flavour drinks.

mustard seeds
Brown and black mustard seeds are used as an essential part of flavouring in Indian cooking. They are usually fried quickly in hot oil until they start to pop and they flavour many pickles, vegetarian dishes, dhals and rice dishes. Mustard seeds have a wonderfully nutty flavour when cooked.

nigella
Also known as black onion seeds, these tiny tear-drop seeds are very aromatic when cooked and are used to flavour breads and pickles.

nutmeg
Nutmeg is the seed of the nutmeg tree. It grows within a lacy cage of mace, inside a fleshy peach-like fruit. It is dried in the sun after harvesting, and is sold both whole and in ground form. Although

very hard to grate, the whole nutmeg may be easily cracked with a hammer. It is best bought whole as the ground form soon loses its fragrance.

okra Known as 'bhindi' in India, okra are the seed pods of a member of the hibiscus family. Choose bright green, firm specimens with no signs of browning.

onion seeds Black in colour and triangular in shape, these are used for both pickles and vegetable curries.

paan Fennel seeds wrapped in betel leaf dressed with calcium paste, held together with a clove and sometimes covered with varq (see below right), for serving at the end of the evening to guests at an Indian party. It acts as a mouth-freshener and coats the mouth with a red colouring.

poppy seeds These dried whole seeds are always better when toasted. They are used to flavour curries. Although they are from the opium poppy, they do not contain opium.

raita A cool dip consisting of yogurt with either onions or cucumber, often served as an accompaniment to hot, spicy dishes.

rosewater The essence of roses, which is used mainly to flavour Indian sweet dishes. Rose petals are also widely used to garnish food.

saffron This highly valued and expensive spice consists of dried stigmas from a special crocus. A flavouring for rice and sweets, it is only used in very small quantities. Saffron is sold both as threads and in powdered form. It has a beautiful flavour and fragrance.

sesame seeds Whole, flat, cream-coloured seeds, these are used to flavour some curries. When ground, they can be made into chutney.

shallots The shallot is widely used in Indian cooking along with onions and spring onions. It is ideally suited to the making of flavourings for sauces because of its subtlety of flavour and the way in which its tender flesh cooks to such softness.

tamarind This is a pod-like fruit from a tall, shady tree, the dried or semi-dried pulp of which is used in Indian cooking. It is usually sold in blocks, and to obtain a purée or paste to use in cooking, it has to be soaked in hot water for a couple of hours, then the pulp can be sieved. It gives food a sour and slightly sweet flavour. However, commercially produced tamarind paste is now widely available.

tandoori masala A commercially produced Indian spice powder mix that will liven up any curry. It can also be used as part of a marinade mixture.

turmeric A rhizome that when dried results in a bright yellow powder. This musky spice is used in small quantities mainly in vegetable and lentil dishes.

varq Edible beaten silver leaf used for decoration purposes. It should be handled very gently as it is extremely light and fragile. It can be bought in sheets from Indian or Pakistani grocers.

soups, starters and snacks

Most of these dishes are usually served as part of a main Indian meal. Here, however, they make easy and elegant starters and snacks. Alternatively, serve with salad and bread for a wonderfully light meal.

paneer tikka

preparation time **5 mins**
cooking time **15 mins**
total time **20 mins** serves **4**

1 tablespoon sunflower oil
15 g/½ oz butter
1 teaspoon cumin seeds
200 g/7 oz chestnut mushrooms, thinly sliced
250 g/8 oz paneer, cut into bite-sized cubes
1 teaspoon sea salt
1 teaspoon freshly ground black pepper
1 teaspoon tandoori masala
handful of chopped fresh coriander leaves
1 tablespoon lemon juice
shredded iceberg lettuce
mint leaves, to garnish

one Heat the oil and butter in a large wok or nonstick frying pan and, when hot, add the cumin and mushrooms. Fry, stirring, for 5–7 mins.
two Add the paneer, salt, pepper, tandoori masala, coriander and lemon juice and cook over a low heat, stirring occasionally, for 7–8 mins.
three To serve, arrange some shredded lettuce on each plate and top with the paneer tikka. Garnish with mint leaves and serve warm.

Ready-prepared paneer is now widely available and can be found in the cheese section of many supermarkets. However, it is simple to make your own (see page 34).

khandvi

preparation time **10 mins**
cooking time **20 mins**
total time **30 mins** serves **4**

2 tablespoons sunflower oil
4 tablespoons gram flour (besan)
1 tablespoon natural yogurt
2 teaspoons sea salt
¼ teaspoon ground turmeric
¼ teaspoon asafoetida
1 teaspoon chilli powder
500 ml/17 fl oz water
8–10 curry leaves
2 teaspoons mustard seeds
1 tablespoon grated fresh coconut
1 tablespoon chopped fresh coriander leaves

one Lightly oil a 30 x 30 cm/12 x 12 inch baking sheet. In a bowl, whisk together the flour, yogurt, salt, turmeric, asafoetida, chilli powder and water.
two Put this mixture into a heavy-based saucepan and bring to the boil, stirring occasionally.
three Reduce the heat and cook, stirring frequently, for 10–15 mins or until thick. Remove from the heat.
four Spoon the mixture on to the baking sheet, spreading it thinly over the surface with the back of a wide spoon. Leave for 5–10 mins to cool, then cut into 2.5 cm/ 1 inch strips and roll up into mini Swiss rolls. Divide between 4 plates.
five Heat the remaining oil in a small saucepan and add the curry leaves and mustard seeds. As soon as the seeds start to pop, spoon the oil over the rolls. Sprinkle over the coconut and coriander and serve.

These lightly spiced rolls are the Indian equivalent of pasta,
but are made from gram flour (besan). Flavoured with coconut,
coriander and mustard seeds, they make a great cold starter.

onion bhajiyas

preparation time **10 mins**, plus resting
cooking time **10 mins**
total time **20 mins** makes **10–12**

1 onion, halved and thinly sliced
5 tablespoons gram flour (besan)
1 tablespoon sunflower oil
2 teaspoons sea salt
1 teaspoon sugar
1 teaspoon lemon juice
1 teaspoon ground cumin
1 fresh green chilli, deseeded and finely
   chopped
1 tablespoon chopped fresh coriander leaves
¾ teaspoon baking powder
2–3 tablespoons water
vegetable oil, for deep-frying
chutney, to serve

one Mix all the ingredients together in a bowl (apart from the oil for deep-frying) and leave the mixture to rest for 10 mins.
two Using your hands, mix well to combine thoroughly.
three Heat the oil in a wok or deep frying pan to 180–190°C (350–375°F) or until a cube of bread browns in 30 seconds, then drop spoonfuls of the mixture into the oil and deep-fry for 1–2 mins until golden. You might have to do this in 2–3 batches.
four Serve hot with chutney.

A popular snack sold on almost every street corner in India, these bhajiyas are delicious served hot with Tamarind and Date Chutney (see page 30) and Coconut Chutney (see page 37).

spiced spinach and carrot pancakes

preparation time **10 mins**
cooking time **20 mins**
total time **30 mins** makes **6**

75 g/3 oz carrots, grated
75 g/3 oz spinach, roughly chopped
1 onion, finely chopped
2 fresh green chillies, deseeded and chopped
1 teaspoon fennel seeds
1 tablespoon ground coriander
100 g/3½ oz gram flour (besan), sieved
50 g/2 oz semolina
1 teaspoon baking powder
300 ml/½ pint water
vegetable oil, for oiling
sea salt

one In a large bowl, mix together the carrots, spinach, onion, chillies, fennel seeds and coriander. Season with salt and set aside.

two Mix together the gram flour, semolina and baking powder and add to the carrot mixture.

three Add the water gradually to the mixture, mixing well with a spoon, until you have a thick batter.

four Lightly oil a nonstick frying pan with oil. When hot, add 2 tablespoons of the mixture and spread with a spatula to make a pancake about 17–18 cm/6½–7 inches in diameter. Cover and cook for 1–2 mins or until the pancake is lightly browned on the base. Flip over and cook for another 2 mins. Repeat with the remaining batter to make 6 pancakes. Serve them hot.

TIP The cooked pancakes can be stored on a lined baking sheet, stacked and interleaved with greaseproof paper, and kept in a low oven 110°C (225°F), Gas Mark ¼, until you are ready to serve them.

These pancakes from Gujerat are made from gram flour (besan) and are known as 'pudlas'. Serve them as a starter with Cucumber and Pomegranate Raita (see page 27).

coriander chicken kebabs

preparation time **10 mins**
cooking time **20 mins**
total time **30 mins** serves **4**

handful of roughly chopped fresh coriander
    leaves
2 tablespoons chopped mint leaves
5 garlic cloves, roughly chopped
2 teaspoons grated fresh root ginger
1 teaspoon ground cumin
1 teaspoon ground coriander
1 fresh green chilli, roughly chopped
2 teaspoons soft brown sugar
400 g/13 oz minced chicken
100 g/3½ oz fresh breadcrumbs
sea salt and pepper
lemon wedges, to serve

one Put the fresh coriander, mint, garlic,
ginger, cumin, ground coriander, chilli and
sugar into a food processor or blender and
process until fairly smooth. Season with
salt and pepper.
two Turn the mixture into a large bowl and
add the chicken and breadcrumbs. Mix well,
using your hands.
three Divide the mixture into 12 and shape
around metal or presoaked wooden
skewers, using your hands.
four Arrange the kebabs on a wire rack
on a baking sheet and bake in a preheated
oven, 200°C (400°F), Gas Mark 6, for
20 mins.
five Serve hot with lemon wedges.

prawn and mango kebabs

preparation time **10 mins**, plus marinating
cooking time **4–5 mins**
total time **15 mins** serves **4**

16 large raw tiger prawns,
    peeled and deveined
1 tablespoon sunflower oil
4 tablespoons lemon juice
2 garlic cloves, crushed
1 teaspoon grated fresh root ginger
1 teaspoon chilli powder
1 tablespoon clear honey
1 teaspoon sea salt
1 large mango, peeled, stoned and cut into
    8 bite-sized pieces
dressed salad, to serve

one Put the prawns into a large bowl and
add the oil, lemon juice, garlic, ginger, chilli
powder, honey and salt. Mix well and
marinate for about 10 mins.
two Remove the prawns from the marinade
and thread 2 prawns alternately between
2 pieces of mango on each of 8 presoaked
wooden skewers.
three Place the skewers under a preheated
hot grill, brush with the remaining marinade
and grill for 2 mins on each side or until the
prawns turn pink and are cooked through.
four Serve 2 skewers on each plate with
some dressed salad.

These kebabs make a colourful and elegant starter.

spicy fish cakes

preparation time **15 mins**
cooking time **15 mins**
total time **30 mins** makes **20**

425 g/14 oz cooked cod fillet
2 potatoes, boiled and mashed
4 spring onions, thinly sliced
2 fresh green chillies, deseeded and finely
   chopped
1 teaspoon grated fresh root ginger
2 garlic cloves, crushed
4 tablespoons chopped fresh coriander leaves
2 eggs
fresh breadcrumbs, for coating
vegetable oil, for frying
sea salt and pepper

one Flake the fish into a bowl and add the potatoes, spring onions, chillies, ginger, garlic and coriander. Season with salt and pepper and add 1 egg. Mix well.

two Shape the fish mixture into 20 small cakes and set aside.

three Beat the remaining egg in a shallow bowl, dip the cakes in the egg and then coat with the breadcrumbs.

four Heat the oil in a large, nonstick frying pan and fry the cakes in batches for 2 mins on each side or until golden brown. Serve the fish cakes hot.

Salmon could easily replace cod in these delicious fish cakes. Serve them with the Mango, Apple and Mint Chutney (see page 35).

tomato and coriander soup

preparation time **10 mins**
cooking time **15 mins**
total time **25 mins** serves **4**

2 tablespoons sunflower oil
4 spring onions
4 curry leaves or 1 bay leaf
400 g/13 oz can chopped tomatoes
1 teaspoon sea salt
1 garlic clove, crushed
1 teaspoon black peppercorns, roughly crushed
3 tablespoons chopped fresh coriander leaves
500 ml/17 fl oz vegetable stock
200 ml/7 fl oz single cream
hot crusty bread, to serve

one Heat the oil in a large saucepan and, when hot, add the spring onions, curry leaves or bay leaf and tomatoes. Cook over a medium heat for 2–3 mins.
two Add the salt, garlic, peppercorns, coriander and stock. Stir and bring to the boil. Cover the pan, reduce the heat and simmer gently for 10 mins.
three Stir in the cream and cook gently for 1–2 mins.
four Ladle the soup into 4 bowls and serve with hot crusty bread.

Use homemade or good-quality vegetable stock to make this flavoursome soup.

These spicy scrambled eggs make a wonderful 'pick-me-up' breakfast or an equally good starter, served with slices of hot buttered toast or toasted ciabatta.

akuri

preparation time **5 mins**
cooking time **6–7 mins**
total time **11–12 mins** serves **4**

15 g/½ oz butter
1 small red onion, finely chopped
1 fresh green chilli, finely sliced
8 organic eggs, lightly beaten
1 tablespoon crème fraîche
1 tomato, finely chopped
1 tablespoon chopped fresh coriander leaves
sea salt
buttered toast, to serve

one Heat the butter in a large, nonstick frying pan and add the onion and chilli. Stir-fry for 1–2 mins.
two Add the eggs, crème fraîche, tomato and coriander. Season with salt and cook over a medium–low heat, stirring frequently, for about 3–4 mins or until the eggs are lightly scrambled and set. Serve hot with buttered toast.

vegetable samosas

preparation time **10 mins**
cooking time **15–20 mins**
total time **25–30 mins** makes **12**

3 large potatoes, boiled and roughly mashed
100 g/3½ oz cooked peas
1 teaspoon cumin seeds
1 teaspoon amchur
    (dried mango powder)
2 fresh green chillies, deseeded and finely
    chopped
1 small red onion, finely chopped
3 tablespoons chopped fresh coriander leaves
1 tablespoon chopped mint leaves
4 tablespoons lemon juice
12 filo pastry sheets, each about
    30 x 18 cm/12 x 7 inches
melted butter, for brushing
sea salt and pepper

one Line a baking sheet with nonstick baking paper. In a large bowl, mix together the potatoes, peas, cumin, amchur, chillies, onion, coriander, mint and lemon juice. Season with salt and pepper to taste and set aside.

two Fold each sheet of filo pastry in half lengthways. Put a large spoonful of the potato mixture at one end and then fold the corner of the pastry over the mixture, covering it in a triangular shape. Continue folding over the triangle of pastry along the length of the pastry strip to make a neat triangular samosa.

three Place the samosas on the baking sheet, brush with melted butter and bake in a preheated oven, 200°C (400°F), Gas Mark 6, for 15–20 mins or until golden.

These crisp savouries can be made in advance and frozen.

They can then be cooked straight from the freezer.

Serve with Coconut Chutney (see page 37).

salads and side dishes

These accompaniments of salads, relishes, pickles and chutneys form an integral part of any Indian meal.

A mildly spiced dressing adds a kick to this nutritious salad.

chickpea salad

preparation time **10 mins**
total time **10 mins** serves **4**

400 g/13 oz can chickpeas, rinsed
    and drained
½ iceberg lettuce, finely shredded
1 cucumber, finely diced
1 small red onion, halved and thinly sliced
4 plum tomatoes, roughly chopped
fresh coriander leaves, to garnish

DRESSING
1 garlic clove, crushed
1 tablespoon olive oil
2 tablespoons lime juice
1 teaspoon caster sugar
½ teaspoon ground cumin
½ teaspoon ground coriander

one Put the chickpeas, lettuce, cucumber, onion and tomatoes into a wide, shallow serving dish or bowl.
two Combine all the dressing ingredients in a small bowl and pour over the salad.
three Toss to mix well and serve garnished with coriander leaves.

potato and red kidney bean salad

preparation time **10 mins**
cooking time **10 mins**
total time **20 mins** serves **4**

400 g/13 oz potatoes, peeled and cut into 2.5
  cm/1 inch cubes
250 ml/8 fl oz Greek yogurt
1 garlic clove, crushed
1 fresh red chilli, thinly sliced
1 teaspoon clear honey
2 tablespoons lime juice
4 tablespoons chopped dill
4 spring onions, thinly sliced
400 g/13 oz can red kidney beans, rinsed and
  drained
sea salt and pepper

one Boil the potatoes in a large saucepan
of water until tender. Drain and set aside.
two In a bowl, mix together the yogurt,
garlic, chilli, honey, lime juice and dill.
Set aside.
three Transfer the potatoes to a salad bowl
and add the spring onions and red kidney
beans. Pour over the yogurt and dill mixture,
season with salt and pepper and serve at
room temperature.

This substantial salad is a superb
variation on a traditional dish.

cucumber and pomegranate raita

preparation time **10 mins**
total time **10 mins** serves **4**

250 ml/8 fl oz natural yogurt
1 cucumber, peeled, deseeded and finely
  chopped
2 tablespoons chopped mint leaves
1 tablespoon chopped fresh coriander leaves
seeds from ½ pomegranate
sea salt and pepper

one Beat the yogurt in a bowl and add the
cucumber, mint, coriander and pomegranate
seeds. Season with salt and pepper and chill
until ready to serve.

This bejewelled raita is the
perfect foil to any hot and
spicy dish.

lobia salad

preparation time **10 mins**
cooking time **8–10 mins**
total time **18–20 mins** serves **4**

2 potatoes, cut into small cubes
100 g/3½ oz green beans, cut into
    2.5 cm/1 inch pieces
400 g/13 oz can black-eyed beans,
    rinsed and drained
4 spring onions, thinly sliced
1 fresh green chilli, deseeded and
    finely chopped
1 tomato, roughly chopped
a handful of mint leaves
hot, toasted Naan (see page 103),
    to serve

DRESSING
2 tablespoons light olive oil
1 tablespoon lemon juice
½ teaspoon chilli powder
1 teaspoon clear honey
sea salt and pepper

one Cook the potatoes and green beans
in a large saucepan of boiling water for
8–10 mins. Drain and place in a large
serving bowl.

two Add the black-eyed beans, spring
onions, chilli, tomato and mint leaves.
Toss to mix well.

three Combine all the dressing ingredients
in a small bowl and mix well. Pour over the
salad, toss to mix well and serve with hot,
toasted Naan (see page 103).

Black-eyed beans feature in this unusual salad.

tamarind and date chutney

preparation time **10 mins**
total time **10 mins** makes about **200 g/7 oz**

200 g/7 oz stoned dried dates,
   roughly chopped
1 tablespoon tamarind paste
1 teaspoon ground cumin
1 teaspoon chilli powder
1 tablespoon tomato ketchup
200 ml/7 fl oz water
sea salt

one Put all the ingredients into a food
processor or blender and process until
fairly smooth.
two Transfer to a serving bowl, cover
and chill until required. It will keep for
up to 3 days in the refrigerator.

This sweet and sour relish makes
a great accompaniment to any
Indian meal, but it is wonderful
in a cheese sandwich as well.

This spicy accompaniment is not for the faint hearted. It is wonderful with rice dishes and can really spice up a sandwich.

lasan chutney

preparation time **5 mins**
total time **5 mins** makes **8–10**

12 garlic cloves, chopped
1 teaspoon chilli powder
2 fresh red chillies, chopped
1 tablespoon vegetable oil
1 teaspoon sea salt
1 tablespoon lime juice

one Put all the ingredients into a food processor or blender and process until smooth. Alternatively, pound to a paste in a mortar with a pestle. This chutney will keep well for up to 2 weeks, stored in an airtight container in the refrigerator.

cauliflower relish

preparation time **10 mins**
cooking time **7–8 mins**
total time **17–18 mins** serves **4**

2 tablespoons vegetable oil
2 teaspoons black mustard seeds
½ teaspoon ground turmeric
½ teaspoon asafoetida
1 small cauliflower, cut into bite-sized pieces
1 red onion, finely chopped
1 fresh green chilli, deseeded and
    finely chopped
lemon juice
sea salt

one Heat the oil in a large, nonstick frying pan and, when hot, add the mustard seeds, turmeric and asafoetida. When the seeds start to pop, add the cauliflower, onion and chilli. Stir-fry for 5 mins, then remove from the heat. The cauliflower should have a bite to it.
two Season with lemon juice and salt to taste. Serve at room temperature.

This is delicious as an accompaniment to kebabs and samosas.

gujarati carrot salad

preparation time **10 mins**
cooking time **2–3 mins**
total time **12–13 mins** serves **4**

500 g/1 lb carrots, coarsely grated
4 tablespoons lemon juice
1 tablespoon clear honey
1 tablespoon vegetable oil
½ teaspoon dried chilli flakes
2 teaspoons black mustard seeds
4 curry leaves
sea salt

one Put the carrots into a serving bowl.
two Mix the lemon juice and honey together
and pour over the carrots. Season with salt.
three Heat the oil in a small saucepan and,
when hot, add the chilli flakes, mustard
seeds and curry leaves. As soon as the
mustard seeds start to pop, remove the
pan from the heat and pour the dressing
over the carrots. Stir well to mix.

This southern Indian relish
is a delicious accompaniment
to any meal.

ginger relish

preparation time **10 mins**
cooking time **2–3 mins**
total time **12–13 mins** serves **4**

2 tablespoons grated fresh root ginger
2 garlic cloves, roughly chopped
1 tablespoon grated fresh coconut or
  2 tablespoons desiccated coconut
2 fresh green chillies, deseeded
1 teaspoon sea salt
1 teaspoon sugar
150 ml/¼ pint natural yogurt, beaten
2 tablespoons vegetable oil
1 teaspoon black mustard seeds
6–8 curry leaves

one Put the ginger, garlic, coconut, chillies,
salt and sugar into a food processor or
blender and process until smooth. Add the
yogurt and process for a few seconds.
two Transfer to a bowl and set aside.
three Heat the oil in a small frying pan and,
when hot, add the mustard seeds and curry
leaves. When the mustard seeds start to
pop, remove the pan from the heat and
pour the spiced oil over the yogurt mixture.
Mix well, cover and chill until required.

Hot spicy oil and honey create a delicious
sweet-and-sour dressing for this simple salad.

paneer

preparation time **2 mins**
cooking time **17–22 mins**, plus setting
total time **14 mins** makes about **150 g/5 oz**

1 litre/1¾ pints full-fat milk
2 tablespoons lemon juice

one Heat the milk in a large saucepan and bring to the boil.
two Add the lemon juice, stirring constantly, until the milk thickens and then begins to curdle.
three Strain the curdled milk through a fine sieve, discarding the whey.
four Turn the cheese out on to a clean chopping board and sandwich with another clean board. Put a heavy weight on top and leave to set for 1 hour. Once set, the cheese can be cut or crumbled into other dishes.

This fresh cheese is now widely available from supermarkets, but it is really special and satisfying when made from scratch. Use in the recipe for Paneer Tikka (see page 14) or serve it on hot Naan (see page 103) with a relish or pickle.

lime pickle

preparation time **10 mins**
cooking time **5 mins**, plus maturing
total time **15 mins** makes **1 jar**

10 limes, each cut into 6 sections
100 g/3½ oz sea salt
1 tablespoon fenugreek seeds
1 tablespoon black mustard seeds
1 tablespoon chilli powder
1 tablespoon ground turmeric
300 ml/½ pint vegetable oil
½ teaspoon asafoetida

one Put the limes into a sterilized jar and cover with the salt.
two In a small frying pan, dry-fry the fenugreek and mustard seeds and then grind them to a powder.
three Add the ground seeds, chilli powder and turmeric to the limes and mix well.
four Heat the oil in a small frying pan until smoking, add the asafoetida and fry for 30 seconds. Pour the oil over the limes and mix well.
five Cover the jar with a clean cloth and leave to mature for 10 days in a bright, warm place. Store the pickle in a tightly covered container. This pickle can be kept for a couple of months.

mango, apple and mint chutney

preparation time **10 mins**
total time **10 mins** serves **4–6**

1 raw green mango, peeled, stoned and
  roughly chopped
1 small apple, peeled, cored and roughly
  chopped
1 teaspoon sea salt
1 tablespoon chopped mint leaves
1 teaspoon mild chilli powder
1 teaspoon soft brown sugar
150 ml/¼ pint water

one Put all the ingredients into a food processor or blender and process until smooth.
two Transfer to a small serving dish, cover and store in the refrigerator until required.

This relish is a tasty accompaniment to many snacks. Try it with Spicy Fish Cakes (see page 20).

This chutney is a terrific accompaniment to Vegetable Samosas (see page 22).

coconut chutney

preparation time **10 mins**
cooking time **2–3 mins**
total time **12–13 mins** serves **4**

100 g/3½ oz grated fresh coconut
3 fresh green chillies, deseeded
1 teaspoon sugar
2 teaspoons grated fresh root ginger
150 ml/¼ pint natural yogurt
2 tablespoons vegetable oil
2 teaspoons black mustard seeds
6–8 curry leaves
sea salt

one Put the coconut, chillies, sugar, ginger and yogurt into a food processor or blender and process until smooth. Transfer to a bowl and set aside.
two Heat the oil in a small frying pan and, when hot, add the mustard seeds and curry leaves. As soon as the seeds start to pop, remove the pan from the heat and pour the spicy oil over the yogurt mixture. Season with salt. Cover and chill until required.

coriander chutney

preparation time **10 mins**
total time **10 mins** makes about **250 g/8 oz**

250 g/8 oz chopped fresh coriander leaves
    and stalks
4 fresh green chillies, deseeded
2 teaspoons grated fresh root ginger
4 garlic cloves, chopped
2 teaspoons caster sugar
1 teaspoon ground cumin
4 tablespoons lemon juice
3 tablespoons chopped mint leaves
200 ml/7 fl oz water
sea salt

one Put all the ingredients into a food processor or blender and process until smooth.
two Transfer the chutney to a serving bowl and keep covered in the refrigerator until ready to use. It will keep for up to 3–4 days in the refrigerator.

This vibrant green chutney is wonderful spread into cucumber sandwiches, adds zing when used as a marinade for grilled fish and livens up any soup or dhal.

meat and poultry

Yogurt is used widely in India for marinating meat and poultry. The yogurt tenderizes the meat and gives a silken texture and wonderful flavour when coupled with other spices and herbs.

tandoori chicken

preparation time **10 mins**,
  plus marinating (optional)
cooking time **20 mins**
total time **30 mins** serves **4**

4 large chicken quarters, skinned
200 ml/7 fl oz natural yogurt
1 teaspoon grated fresh root ginger
2 garlic cloves, crushed
1 teaspoon garam masala
2 teaspoons ground coriander
¼ teaspoon ground turmeric
1 tablespoon tandoori masala
4 tablespoons lemon juice
1 tablespoon vegetable oil
sea salt
lime or lemon wedges, to garnish

one Put the chicken into a non-metallic, shallow, ovenproof dish and make 3 deep slashes in each piece, to allow the flavours to penetrate. Set aside.

two In a bowl, mix together the yogurt, ginger, garlic, garam masala, ground coriander, turmeric, tandoori masala, lemon juice and oil. Season with salt and spread the mixture over the chicken pieces to cover. Cover and marinate overnight in the refrigerator, if time allows.

three Bake the chicken in a preheated oven, 240°C (475°F), Gas Mark 9, for 20 mins or until cooked through. Remove from the oven and serve hot, garnished with lime or lemon wedges.

The flavour of this chicken dish when cooked in a
tandoor (clay oven) is sublime. However, this recipe
comes very close to capturing the real thing.

ginger chicken

preparation time **10 mins**
cooking time **15 mins**
total time **25 mins** serves **4**

250 ml/8 fl oz natural yogurt
1 tablespoon grated fresh root ginger
2 garlic cloves, crushed
1 tablespoon chilli powder
1 tablespoon ground coriander
2 teaspoons ground cumin
2 tablespoons vegetable oil
250 g/8 oz chicken thighs, skinned, boned
    and cut into bite-sized pieces
150 ml/¼ pint chicken stock
sea salt and pepper
chopped fresh coriander leaves, to garnish

one In a bowl, mix together the yogurt, ginger, garlic, chilli powder, ground coriander and cumin. Season with salt and pepper.

two Heat the oil in a large, nonstick frying pan and, when hot, add the chicken. Stir-fry for 4–5 mins or until sealed.

three Add the yogurt mixture and the stock. Bring to the boil, cover and cook gently for 8–10 mins, stirring frequently, until the chicken is tender and cooked through. Serve hot, garnished with fresh coriander.

chettinad chicken

preparation time **10 mins**
cooking time **20 mins**
total time **30 mins** serves **4**

2 tablespoons sunflower oil
1 onion, halved and thinly sliced
10 curry leaves
1 fresh green chilli, chopped
2 garlic cloves, crushed
2 teaspoons grated fresh root ginger
1 teaspoon ground coriander
450 g/14½ oz chicken thighs, skinned,
    boned and cut into bite-sized pieces
250 ml/8 fl oz chicken stock
1 teaspoon garam masala
sea salt and pepper

one Heat the oil in a large, nonstick frying pan and, when hot, add the onion, curry leaves and chilli. Fry, stirring constantly, until the onions are soft. Add the garlic and ginger and stir-fry for 1–2 mins.
two Add the coriander and chicken and fry, stirring constantly, for 2–3 mins. Pour in the stock and add the garam masala. Cover and cook gently for 10–12 mins or until the chicken is cooked through. Season with salt and pepper and serve hot.

This dish comes from southern India and should be eaten with rice and yogurt.

chicken achaari

preparation time **10 mins**
cooking time **12–15 mins**
total time **22–25 mins** serves **4**

2 tablespoons vegetable oil
½ teaspoon cumin seeds
½ teaspoon black mustard seeds
½ teaspoon onion seeds
½ teaspoon fennel seeds
½ teaspoon coriander seeds
1 teaspoon grated fresh root ginger
2 garlic cloves, finely chopped
1 onion, finely chopped
1 teaspoon chilli powder
200 ml/7 fl oz chicken stock
2 tablespoons tomato purée
250 g/8 oz chicken thighs, skinned, boned
   and cut into bite-sized pieces
sea salt and pepper
chopped fresh red chillies, to garnish

one Heat the oil in a wok or large frying pan.
When hot, add all the spice seeds and stir-fry
for 1 min.
two Add the ginger, garlic, onion, chilli powder,
stock and tomato purée and stir for 1 min.
three Add the chicken and bring to the boil.
Reduce the heat, cover the pan and simmer
for 5–7 mins or until the chicken is tender
and cooked through. Season with salt and
pepper and garnish with chopped chillies.

coconut chicken

preparation time **10 mins**
cooking time **20 mins**
total time **30 mins** serves **4**

1 tablespoon ground almonds
1 tablespoon desiccated coconut
125 ml/4 fl oz coconut milk
150 ml/¼ pint fromage frais
2 teaspoons ground coriander
1 teaspoon chilli powder
2 garlic cloves, crushed
2 teaspoons grated fresh root ginger
2 teaspoons sea salt
1 tablespoon vegetable oil
400 g/13 oz chicken thighs, skinned, boned
   and cut into bite-sized pieces
4 cardamom pods
1 teaspoon crushed red chilli flakes
3 tablespoons chopped fresh coriander
plain boiled rice, to serve

one In a small frying pan, dry-fry the almonds
and coconut, stirring constantly, until light
brown. Transfer to a mixing bowl and add the
coconut milk, fromage frais, ground coriander,
chilli powder, garlic, ginger and salt. Stir to
mix well.
two Heat the oil in a large, nonstick frying
pan and fry the chicken and cardamom for
2–3 mins.
three Stir in the coconut mixture and chilli
flakes, cover and cook gently for 10–12 mins,
stirring occasionally. Add the fresh coriander,
stir and serve hot, with plain boiled rice.

This is an excellent dish for
a family supper or a mid-week
meal with friends.

bombay chicken
masala

preparation time **10 mins**
cooking time **15 mins**
total time **25 mins** serves **4**

1 onion, roughly chopped
6 fresh green chillies, deseeded and chopped
6 garlic cloves, chopped
2 teaspoons grated fresh root ginger
1 tablespoon ground coriander
2 teaspoons ground cumin
large bunch of fresh coriander leaves, roughly
   chopped
150 ml/¼ pint water
2 tablespoons vegetable oil
400 g/13 oz boneless chicken breast,
   cut into strips
250 ml/8 fl oz chicken stock
sea salt and pepper

one Put the onion, chillies, garlic, ginger,
ground coriander, cumin, fresh coriander
and water into a food processor or blender
and process to a fairly smooth green paste.
Set aside.

two Heat the oil in a large, nonstick frying
pan and add the green paste. Fry, stirring
constantly, for 1 min, then add the chicken.
Fry, stirring, for 2–3 mins, then add the
stock. Mix well, cover and cook gently for
10–12 mins or until the chicken is tender.
Season with salt and pepper and serve hot.

cashew nut chicken

preparation time **10 mins**
cooking time **20 mins**
total time **30 mins** serves **4**

1 onion, roughly chopped
4 tablespoons tomato purée
50 g/2 oz cashew nuts
2 teaspoons garam masala
2 garlic cloves, crushed
1 tablespoon lemon juice
¼ teaspoon ground turmeric
2 teaspoons sea salt
1 tablespoon natural yogurt
2 tablespoons vegetable oil
3 tablespoons chopped fresh coriander leaves,
   plus extra to garnish
50 g/2 oz ready-to-eat dried apricots, chopped
500 g/1 lb chicken thighs, skinned,
   boned and cut into bite-sized pieces
300 ml/½ pint chicken stock
toasted cashew nuts, to garnish

one Put the onion, tomato purée, cashew nuts, garam masala, garlic, lemon juice, turmeric, salt and yogurt into a food processor or blender and process until fairly smooth. Set aside.

two Heat the oil in a large, nonstick frying pan and, when hot, pour in the spice mixture. Fry, stirring, for 2 mins over a medium heat. Add half the chopped coriander, the apricots and chicken to the pan and stir-fry for 1 min.

three Pour in the stock, cover and simmer for 10–12 mins or until the chicken is cooked through and tender. Stir in the remaining chopped coriander and serve, garnished with toasted cashew nuts and extra coriander.

kheema aloo

preparation time **10 mins**
cooking time **15–20 mins**
total time **25–30 mins** serves **4**

1 tablespoon vegetable oil
4 cardamom pods
1 cinnamon stick
3 cloves
2 onions, finely chopped
375 g/12 oz minced lamb
2 teaspoons garam masala
2 teaspoons chilli powder
2 garlic cloves, crushed
2 teaspoons grated fresh root ginger
2 teaspoons sea salt
200 g/7 oz potatoes, cut into 1 cm/
    ½ inch cubes
200 g/7 oz can chopped tomatoes
100 ml/3½ fl oz hot water
4 tablespoons chopped fresh coriander leaves
boiled rice or bread, to serve

one Heat the oil in a nonstick frying pan and, when hot, add the cardamom, cinnamon and cloves. Fry for 1 min, then add the onions and fry, stirring, for 3–4 mins.

two Add the lamb to the pan with the garam masala, chilli powder, garlic, ginger and salt. Stir well to break up the mince and fry for 5–7 mins.

three Add the potatoes, tomatoes and the hot water, cover and simmer gently for 5 mins or until the potatoes are tender. Stir in the coriander and serve hot with boiled rice or bread.

This spicy minced lamb dish with potatoes is gently flavoured
with cardamom, cinnamon and cloves. Minced lamb may be
replaced with minced chicken or pork, if liked.

seekh kebabs

preparation time **10 mins**,
   plus chilling (optional)
cooking time **10 mins**
total time **20 mins** makes **12**

2 fresh green chillies, deseeded and finely
   chopped
1 teaspoon grated fresh root ginger
2 garlic cloves, crushed
3 tablespoons chopped fresh coriander leaves
2 tablespoons chopped mint leaves
1 teaspoon cumin seeds
1 tablespoon vegetable oil, plus extra for oiling
½ teaspoon ground cloves
½ teaspoon ground cardamom seeds
450 g/14½ oz minced beef
sea salt

one Put the chillies, ginger, garlic, coriander, mint, cumin, oil, cloves and cardamom into a food processor or blender and process until fairly smooth. Transfer to a mixing bowl, add the beef and season with salt. Mix well, using your hands. Divide the mixture into 12 portions, cover and chill for 30 mins, if time allows.

two Lightly oil 12 flat metal skewers and shape the kebab mixture around each skewer, forming a sausage shape.

three Place the kebabs under a preheated hot grill and cook for 3–4 mins on each side or until cooked through and browned.

These kebabs are a popular street food in India. Barbecued over
charcoal braziers, they are eaten with red onions, mint and hot bread.

lamb kebabs

preparation time **10 mins**
cooking time **20 mins**
total time **30 mins** makes **12**

450 g/14½ oz minced lamb
1 small red onion, finely chopped
3 tablespoons chopped fresh coriander leaves
2 tablespoons chopped mint leaves
2 fresh green chillies, chopped
2 garlic cloves, crushed
2 teaspoons grated fresh root ginger
1 egg, lightly beaten
sea salt and pepper

one Line a baking sheet with baking paper and set aside.
two Put the lamb, onion, coriander, mint, chillies, garlic, ginger and egg into a large bowl, season with salt and pepper and, using your hands, mix until thoroughly blended. Divide the mixture into 12 portions and form each one into a round shape.
three Place the kebabs on the baking sheet and bake in a preheated oven, 200°C (400°F), Gas Mark 6, for 20 mins or until golden brown. Serve hot.

These kebabs are a spicy alternative to the hamburger. They work wonderfully stuffed in pitta bread with salad and could be cooked on a barbecue.

kashmiri lamb chops

preparation time **10 mins**,
  plus marinating (optional)
cooking time **8–12 mins**
total time **18–22 mins** serves **4**

150 ml/¼ pint natural yogurt
1 teaspoon chilli powder
2 teaspoons grated fresh root ginger
2 garlic cloves, crushed
1 tablespoon sunflower oil, plus extra
  for oiling
8 lamb loin chops
sea salt and pepper

one Mix together the yogurt, chilli powder, ginger, garlic and oil in a large bowl and season with salt and pepper.
two Add the chops to this mixture and coat them thoroughly. Cover and marinate for 3–10 hours in the refrigerator, if time allows.
three Place the chops on a lightly oiled grill pan. Cook under a preheated hot grill for 4–6 mins on each side or until tender.

beef chilli fry

preparation time **10 mins**
cooking time **15–20 mins**
total time **25–30 mins** serves **4**

3 tablespoons vegetable oil
6 large fresh green chillies, slit in half
1 teaspoon cumin seeds
4 curry leaves
2 teaspoons grated fresh root ginger
1 teaspoon chilli powder
1 teaspoon ground coriander
2 garlic cloves, crushed
2 teaspoons sea salt
2 onions, finely chopped
450 g/14½ oz beef sirloin steak,
   cut into thin strips
4 tablespoons lemon juice
2 tablespoons chopped mint
1 tablespoon chopped fresh coriander leaves

one Heat the oil in a large, nonstick frying pan and, when hot, add the chillies. Fry for 1 min, then remove with a slotted spoon and set aside.

two Add the cumin, curry leaves, ginger, chilli powder, ground coriander, garlic, salt and onions to the pan and stir-fry for 1–2 mins, stirring constantly.

three Add the beef strips and stir-fry for 8–10 mins or until cooked through.

four Add the lemon juice, mint and fresh coriander, return the chillies to the pan and fry, stirring, for 1–2 mins. Serve immediately.

spicy pork patties

preparation time **10 mins**, plus chilling
cooking time **6–8 mins**
total time **16–18 mins** makes **12**

450 g/14½ oz minced pork
3 teaspoons hot curry paste
3 tablespoons fresh breadcrumbs
1 small onion, finely chopped
2 tablespoons lime juice
2 tablespoons chopped fresh coriander leaves
1 fresh red chilli, finely chopped
2 teaspoons soft brown sugar
sunflower oil, for frying
sea salt and pepper

TO SERVE
natural yogurt
Coriander Chutney (see page 37)

one Put the pork, curry paste, breadcrumbs, onion, lime juice, coriander, chilli and sugar into a large bowl and, using your hands, mix until thoroughly blended. Season with salt and pepper, cover and chill for 30 mins or until ready to cook.
two Divide the mixture into 12 portions and shape each one into a flat, round patty.
three Heat the oil in a large, nonstick frying pan and cook the patties over a medium heat for 3–4 mins on each side or until cooked through. Remove with a slotted spoon and drain on kitchen paper. Serve hot with yogurt and Coriander Chutney (see page 37).

fish and shellfish

Healthy, delicious and really quick
to cook, these seafood recipes are
influenced by the various different
coastal regions of India.

salmon in banana leaves

preparation time **10 mins**
cooking time **15 mins**
total time **25 mins** serves **4**

large bunch of fresh coriander leaves, roughly
   chopped
3 tablespoons chopped mint leaves
2 garlic cloves, crushed
1 teaspoon grated fresh root ginger
4 fresh red chillies, deseeded and chopped
2 teaspoons ground cumin
1 teaspoon ground coriander
2 teaspoons soft brown sugar
2 tablespoons lime juice
150 ml/¼ pint coconut milk
4 thick salmon fillets, skinned
4 squares of banana leaf (each approximately
   30 x 30 cm/12 x 12 inches)
sea salt and pepper

one Put the fresh coriander, mint, garlic, ginger, chillies, cumin, ground coriander, sugar, lime juice and coconut milk into a food processor or blender and blend until fairly smooth. Season with salt and pepper and set aside.

two Place each salmon fillet on a square of banana leaf and spoon some of the herb and spice mixture over it. Carefully cover the fish with the leaf to make a neat parcel and secure with wooden skewers.

three Place the parcels on a large baking sheet and bake in a preheated oven, 200°C (400°F), Gas Mark 6, for 15 mins.

four Remove the parcels from the oven, place on a serving plate and open the packages at the table.

TIP To make the banana leaves supple, hold them over an open flame until they go a bright green. They will then be easier to handle. If you cannot get hold of banana leaves, use baking paper instead.

All the aromas of the herbs and spices are unleashed
when you open up the banana leaf packages.

spicy pan-fried cod

preparation time **10 mins**
cooking time **15–20 mins**
total time **25–30 mins** serves **4**

2 tablespoons gram flour (besan)
1 tablespoon plain flour
1 tablespoon amchur (dried mango powder)
2 teaspoons chilli powder
1 tablespoon cumin seeds
1 teaspoon grated fresh root ginger
1 garlic clove, crushed
2 teaspoons sea salt
4 thick cod fillets, skinned
sunflower oil, for frying

one In a bowl, mix together the gram flour, plain flour, amchur, chilli powder, cumin, ginger, garlic and salt.
two Place the fish on a chopping board and dust with the spiced flour on both sides, to coat evenly.
three Heat the oil in a large, nonstick frying pan and, when hot, fry the fish in 2 batches for 3–4 mins on each side or until cooked through. Drain on kitchen paper. Serve hot.

In India, this dish would be prepared with a tropical fish, such as pomfret, but it is also a tasty way to cook cod.

fish mollee

preparation time **10 mins**
cooking time **15 mins**
total time **25 mins** serves **4**

875 g/1¾ lb thick, skinless cod or halibut fillets,
    cut into 4 cm/1½ inch pieces
4 tablespoons lemon juice
1 tablespoon vegetable oil
1 onion, finely chopped
3 garlic cloves, crushed
1 teaspoon ground turmeric
4 fresh green chillies, deseeded and finely
    chopped
300 ml/½ pint coconut milk
1 tablespoon white wine vinegar
sea salt and pepper

This mild Anglo-Indian curry is
wonderful served with boiled
rice, Lime Pickle (see page 35)
and poppadoms.

one Put the fish into a large, shallow,
non-metallic dish, season with salt and
squeeze over the lemon juice. Cover
and set aside.
two Heat the oil in a large, nonstick
frying pan and add the onion and garlic.
Fry, stirring constantly, for 2–3 mins, then
add the turmeric, chillies and coconut milk.
Cook briskly for 2–3 mins.
three Add the fish. Stir carefully and
add the vinegar. Cover the pan and cook
for 7–10 mins or until the fish is cooked
through. Season with salt and pepper
and serve hot.

VARIATION Substitute raw tiger prawns
for the fish. Cook until the prawns have
just turned pink.

crab malabar-hill

preparation time **10 mins**
cooking time **5–6 mins**
total time **15–16 mins** serves **4**

2 tablespoons vegetable oil
3 garlic cloves, finely chopped
2 teaspoons finely chopped fresh root ginger
6 spring onions, very thinly sliced
3 fresh red chillies, deseeded and finely sliced
625 g/1¼ lb fresh white crab meat
grated rind and juice of 1 lime
4 tablespoons chopped fresh coriander leaves
2 tablespoons chopped mint leaves
sea salt and pepper
crisp lettuce leaves, to serve

one Heat the oil in a large wok or nonstick frying pan and, when hot, add the garlic, ginger, spring onions and chillies. Fry, stirring constantly, for 2–3 mins.
two Add the crab meat, lime rind and juice, coriander and mint. Stir-fry for 2–3 mins, season with salt and pepper and serve hot on crisp lettuce leaves.

This dish featured regularly on the menu at
my home in Malabar-hill, Bombay.

baked coconut trout

preparation time **10 mins**
cooking time **15 mins**
total time **25 mins** serves **4**

4 small trout, cleaned
4 tablespoons lemon juice
2 garlic cloves, crushed
1 teaspoon grated fresh root ginger
1 tablespoon ground almonds
3 tablespoons tomato purée
2 fresh green chillies, finely chopped
1 teaspoon garam masala
200 ml/7 fl oz coconut milk
1 tablespoon chopped fresh coriander leaves
1 tablespoon vegetable oil
sea salt and pepper
boiled rice and salad, to serve

one Put the fish into a large, non-metallic, ovenproof dish, season with salt and squeeze over the lemon juice.

two Mix together the garlic, ginger, almonds, tomato purée, chillies, garam masala, coconut milk, coriander and oil. Season with salt and pepper and pour over the fish to coat well.

three Bake the fish in a preheated oven, 200°C (400°F), Gas Mark 6, for 15 mins until it is cooked through. Serve hot with rice and a salad.

My idea of heaven would be sitting under the palms by the sea and making a meal of this fried fish, with dhal, rice and a salad.

kerala-style fried fish

preparation time **10 mins**,
   plus marinating (optional)
cooking time **12 mins**
total time **22 mins** serves **4**

1 small onion, finely grated to a paste
2 garlic cloves, finely grated
2 teaspoons ground coriander
1 teaspoon hot chilli powder
1 teaspoon pepper
1 tablespoon lemon juice
2 teaspoons sea salt
1 tablespoon sunflower oil, plus extra
   for frying
4 skinless plaice fillets
150 g/5 oz plain flour

one Put the onion, garlic, coriander, chilli powder, pepper, lemon juice, salt and the 1 tablespoon of oil into a bowl and mix together thoroughly to form a paste. Put the fish into a large, non-metallic, shallow dish and smear with the paste to coat evenly. Cover and marinate for 1 hour in the refrigerator, if time allows.

two Place the flour on a large plate and, when ready to cook, coat the fish fillets in it. Shake off any excess flour.

three Heat the oil in a large, nonstick frying pan and shallow-fry the fish in batches for about 2–3 mins on each side until it is cooked through. Drain on kitchen paper and serve hot.

spiced mussel curry

preparation time **10 mins**
cooking time **10–12 mins**
total time **20–22 mins** serves **4**

1 kg/2 lb live mussels
1 tablespoon vegetable oil
1 onion, finely chopped
4 garlic cloves, crushed
3 fresh green chillies, finely chopped
1 teaspoon ground turmeric
100 ml/3½ fl oz white wine vinegar
400 ml/14 fl oz can coconut milk
2 teaspoons sugar
4 tablespoons chopped fresh coriander leaves
sea salt and pepper
freshly grated coconut, to garnish
crusty white bread, to serve

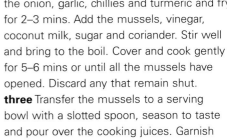

one Rinse the mussels under cold running water and scrape off any beards. Discard any that are open or that do not close when sharply tapped. Drain and set aside.
two Heat the oil in a large saucepan, add the onion, garlic, chillies and turmeric and fry for 2–3 mins. Add the mussels, vinegar, coconut milk, sugar and coriander. Stir well and bring to the boil. Cover and cook gently for 5–6 mins or until all the mussels have opened. Discard any that remain shut.
three Transfer the mussels to a serving bowl with a slotted spoon, season to taste and pour over the cooking juices. Garnish with grated coconut and serve with crusty white bread to mop up the juices.

This is best made with live mussels, available
from supermarkets and fishmongers.

prawns with curry leaves and fenugreek

preparation time **10 mins**
cooking time **12–15 mins**
total time **22–25 mins** serves **4**

1 tablespoon sunflower oil
2 onions, halved and thinly sliced
8–10 curry leaves
1 teaspoon nigella
1 fresh red chilli, finely sliced
625 g/1¼ lb raw tiger prawns,
    peeled and deveined
2 teaspoons grated fresh root ginger
2 teaspoons sea salt
1 tablespoon fenugreek leaves
1 tablespoon lemon juice
hot white bread, to serve

one Heat the oil in a large, nonstick frying pan, add the onions, curry leaves and nigella and stir-fry for 3 mins.
two Add the chilli and prawns and fry, stirring constantly, for 5–7 mins. Add the ginger and salt and fry, stirring, for another minute or until the prawns turn pink and are just cooked through.
three Finally, add the fenugreek leaves and lemon juice and cook for 1–2 mins. Remove from the heat and serve hot with hot white bread.

The marriage of the aromatic curry leaves and pungent fresh
fenugreek leaves gives this prawn curry a distinctive flavour.

monkfish kebabs

preparation time **10 mins**, plus marinating
cooking time **8–10 mins**
total time **18–20 mins** serves **4**

1 kg/2 lb monkfish fillet, cut into
    4 cm/1½ inch cubes
200 ml/7 fl oz natural yogurt
4 tablespoons lemon juice
3 garlic cloves, crushed
2 teaspoons grated fresh root ginger
1 teaspoon hot chilli powder
1 teaspoon ground cumin
1 teaspoon ground coriander
2 fresh red chillies, finely sliced
sea salt and pepper

TO GARNISH
chopped fresh coriander leaves
lime slices
sliced red chillies

one Put the monkfish cubes into a non-metallic bowl.

two In a small bowl, mix together the yogurt, lemon juice, garlic, ginger, chilli powder, cumin, ground coriander and chillies and season with salt and pepper. Pour this over the fish, cover and marinate in the refrigerator overnight, if time allows.

three Lift the fish out of the marinade and thread on to 8 flat metal skewers. Place on a grill rack and cook under a preheated hot grill for 8–10 mins, turning once, until the fish is cooked through. Serve hot, garnished with chopped fresh coriander, lime slices and chilli slices.

Monkfish is quite meaty and holds its shape well
when cooked, so it is perfect for kebabs.

baked spiced halibut

preparation time **10 mins**,
  plus marinating (optional)
cooking time **20 mins**
total time **30 mins** serves **4**

4 thick halibut steaks (about 200 g/7 oz each)
1 small onion, finely chopped
2 garlic cloves, crushed
1 teaspoon grated fresh root ginger
2 teaspoons ground cumin
1 teaspoon ground coriander
4 tablespoons lemon juice
1 teaspoon dried red chilli flakes
250 ml/8 fl oz natural yogurt
sea salt and pepper
lemon wedges and fresh coriander leaves,
  to garnish

one Put the halibut steaks into a large,
shallow, metallic, ovenproof dish.
two Put the onion, garlic, ginger, cumin,
ground coriander, lemon juice and chilli
flakes into a food processor or blender with
half the yogurt and process until smooth.
Add the remaining yogurt and blend again.
Season with salt and pepper.
three Pour the yogurt marinade over the fish,
using your hands to coat the fish thoroughly
on both sides. Cover and marinate in the
refrigerator overnight, if time allows.
four Cover the dish with foil and bake in a
preheated oven, 190°C (375°F), Gas Mark 5,
for 10 mins, then remove the foil and bake
for another 7–10 mins or until the fish is
cooked through. Serve hot, garnished with
lemon wedges and fresh coriander.

tomato fish curry

preparation time **10 mins**
cooking time **15 mins**
total time **25 mins** serves **4**

2 tablespoons vegetable oil
1 onion, finely chopped
4 garlic cloves, sliced
1 teaspoon grated fresh root ginger
½ teaspoon ground turmeric
1 teaspoon chilli powder
1 teaspoon ground cumin
2 teaspoons ground coriander
1 teaspoon garam masala
500 g/1 lb thick white fish fillets, cut into
  2.5 cm/1 inch pieces
400 g/13 oz can chopped tomatoes
2 teaspoons sea salt
2 teaspoons sugar
boiled rice, to serve

one Heat the oil in a large, nonstick frying
pan, add the onion and fry until soft and
lightly browned. Add the garlic, ginger,
turmeric, chilli powder, cumin, coriander
and garam masala and fry for 30 seconds.
two Add the fish to the pan and stir gently
for 1 min.
three Add the tomatoes, salt and sugar and
stir carefully. Cover and simmer gently for
7–10 mins or until the fish is cooked through.
Serve hot with rice.

Any firm white fish, such as cod
or haddock, is suitable for this
aromatic curry.

Cooked with lots of onions – 'dopiaza' – this dish has a rich and spicy flavour.

prawn dopiaza

preparation time **10 mins**
cooking time **20 mins**
total time **30 mins** serves **4**

2 tablespoons vegetable oil
3 onions, thinly sliced
1 teaspoon onion seeds
1 teaspoon grated garlic
1 teaspoon grated fresh root ginger
1 teaspoon chilli powder
½ teaspoon ground turmeric
625 g/1¼ lb raw tiger prawns, peeled
    and deveined
2 tablespoons chopped fresh coriander leaves
1 tablespoon lemon juice
sea salt and pepper

one Heat the oil in a large, nonstick frying pan and add the onions. Cook over a medium heat, stirring occasionally, for about 7–10 mins until golden brown.
two Add the onion seeds, garlic, ginger, chilli powder and turmeric and stir-fry for 1–2 mins.
three Add the prawns, coriander and lemon juice and season with salt and pepper. Cover the pan and cook gently for 5–7 mins or until the prawns are cooked through. Serve hot.

goan prawn curry

preparation time **10 mins**
cooking time **15 mins**
total time **25 mins** serves **4**

1 teaspoon chilli powder
1 tablespoon paprika
½ teaspoon ground turmeric
4 garlic cloves, crushed
2 teaspoons grated fresh root ginger
2 tablespoons ground coriander
1 teaspoon ground cumin
2 teaspoons jaggery or soft brown sugar
300 ml/½ pint water
400 ml/14 fl oz can coconut milk
2 teaspoons sea salt
1 tablespoon tamarind paste
625 g/1¼ lb raw tiger prawns
boiled white rice, to serve

one Put the chilli powder, paprika, turmeric, garlic, ginger, coriander, cumin, the jaggery or sugar and the water into a bowl. Mix well and transfer to a large saucepan. Bring this mixture to the boil, then reduce the heat, cover and simmer gently for 7–8 mins.
two Add the coconut milk, salt and tamarind paste and bring to a simmer.
three Stir in the prawns and cook briskly until they turn pink and are just cooked through. Serve hot, accompanied by boiled white rice.

I prepared a version of this extremely simple and wonderful
recipe on a boat off the Goan coast, for one of Madhur Jaffrey's
television series. I have cooked it regularly since then.

vegetables
and pulses

Fresh vegetables and pulses
form the basis of day-to-day
Indian cooking. A wide
variety of common and
slightly unusual vegetables
are used in these recipes.

tarka dhal

preparation time **5 mins**, plus soaking
cooking time **25 mins**
total time **30 mins** serves **4**

250 g/8 oz red split lentils
1 litre/1¾ pints hot water
200 g/7 oz can chopped tomatoes
2 fresh green chillies, deseeded and finely
    chopped (optional)
¼ teaspoon ground turmeric
2 teaspoons grated fresh root ginger
4 tablespoons chopped fresh coriander
sea salt and pepper

TARKA
1 tablespoon sunflower oil
2 teaspoons black mustard seeds
1 teaspoon cumin seeds
2 garlic cloves, thinly sliced
1 dried red chilli

one Soak the lentils in boiling water to
cover for 10 mins. Drain and put into a large
saucepan with the hot water. Bring to the
boil over a high heat, spooning off any scum
that comes to the surface. Reduce the heat
and cook for 20 mins or until soft and tender.
two Drain the lentils and process to a
purée in a food processor or using a hand-
held electric whisk. Return the purée to
the rinsed pan with the tomatoes, chillies,
turmeric, ginger and coriander. Season with
salt and pepper, return to the heat and
simmer gently.
three Meanwhile, make the tarka. Heat
the oil in a small, nonstick frying pan
and, when hot, add all the ingredients.
Fry, stirring constantly, for 1–2 mins.
four Remove the tarka from the heat
and pour on to the cooked dhal. Stir and
serve hot.

spinach
with besan

preparation time **5 mins**
cooking time **20 mins**
total time **25 mins** serves **4**

1 tablespoon vegetable oil
1 teaspoon mustard seeds
2 garlic cloves, finely chopped
250 g/8 oz baby spinach
1 teaspoon chilli powder
1 teaspoon ground cumin
2 teaspoons ground coriander
1 fresh green chilli, chopped
2 tablespoons gram flour (besan)
4 tablespoons water
dash of lemon juice
sea salt

one Heat the oil in a large frying pan and,
when hot, add the mustard seeds, garlic and
spinach. Sauté for 5 mins, then add the chilli
powder, cumin, coriander and chilli.
two Mix together the gram flour and water
and pour into the spinach mixture. Stir and
cook for 5 mins until the spinach and gram
flour are well blended. Cover and cook
gently for another 8–10 mins.
three Season with salt and squeeze over
some lemon juice. Serve hot.

This is the ultimate basic Indian comfort food. Tarka is the process
by which food is given the final seasoning, in this case with spiced oil,
to flavour the dish. I love to eat this dhal with basmati rice, natural
yogurt and hot green mango pickle or Lime Pickle (see page 35).

stuffed spiced okra

preparation time **10 mins,** plus resting
cooking time **15–18 mins**
total time **25–28 mins** serves **4**

250 g/8 oz large fresh okra, trimmed
1 teaspoon grated fresh root ginger
1 teaspoon ground cumin
1 tablespoon amchur (dried mango powder)
½ teaspoon chilli powder
¼ teaspoon ground turmeric
2 teaspoons vegetable oil
3 tablespoons cornflour
sea salt and pepper
vegetable oil, for deep-frying

one With a sharp knife, make a lengthways slit in each okra, being careful not to cut right through.

two In a small bowl, mix together the ginger, cumin, amchur, chilli powder and turmeric. Add the oil, season with salt and pepper and stir to mix well. Set aside for 10–15 mins to rest.

three Using your finger and a small teaspoon, carefully part the slits in the okra and fill each one with some of the spiced filling.

four Put the okra into a polythene bag with the cornflour and shake gently to coat them evenly.

five Pour at least 4 cm/1½ inches of oil into a wok or deep frying pan and heat. When hot, deep-fry the okra in 3 batches for about 5–6 mins or until they are lightly browned and crisp. Drain on kitchen paper and serve hot.

This unusual accompaniment would go down as well with Western grills as it does with other Indian dishes.

mutter paneer

preparation time **10 mins**
cooking time **20 mins**
total time **30 mins** serves **4**

2 tablespoons vegetable oil
1 teaspoon mustard seeds
1 teaspoon cumin seeds
1 cinnamon stick or piece of cassia
1 dried red Kashmiri chilli
4 cloves
4 cardamom pods
1 onion, finely chopped
2 teaspoons grated fresh root ginger
1 fresh green chilli, chopped
4 garlic cloves, crushed
1 teaspoon hot chilli powder
1 teaspoon garam masala
1 teaspoon ground turmeric
2 tablespoons dhana-jeera (see page 9)
2 teaspoons soft brown sugar or jaggery
200 g/7 oz can chopped tomatoes
200 g/7 oz paneer, cubed or crumbled
450 g/14½ oz frozen peas
175 ml/6 fl oz water
4 tablespoons crème fraîche
sea salt and pepper
fresh coriander leaves, to garnish

one Heat the oil in a large saucepan and, when hot, add the mustard and cumin seeds, cinnamon or cassia, dried chilli, cloves and cardamom. Stir-fry until the seeds start to pop, then add the onion and stir-fry for 4–5 mins. Add the ginger, fresh chilli, garlic, chilli powder, garam masala, turmeric, dhana-jeera and sugar or jaggery and stir well.

two Add the tomatoes, paneer, peas and water. Simmer gently for 10 mins, stirring occasionally.

three Stir in the crème fraîche and season with salt and pepper. Serve hot, garnished with coriander leaves.

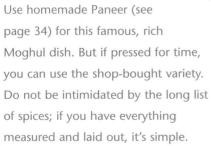

Use homemade Paneer (see page 34) for this famous, rich Moghul dish. But if pressed for time, you can use the shop-bought variety. Do not be intimidated by the long list of spices; if you have everything measured and laid out, it's simple.

mushroom korma

preparation time **10 mins**
cooking time **18–20 mins**
total time **28–30 mins** serves **4**

2 tablespoons vegetable oil
1 onion, finely chopped
1 teaspoon grated fresh root ginger
1 fresh green chilli, chopped
500 g/1 lb large button or chestnut
   mushrooms, halved
1 teaspoon chilli powder
½ teaspoon ground turmeric
2 teaspoons ground cumin
1 tablespoon ground coriander
200 g/7 oz can chopped tomatoes
1 teaspoon sugar
3 tablespoons single cream
2 tablespoons chopped fresh coriander leaves
sea salt and pepper

one Heat the oil in a large saucepan and fry
the onion until soft and lightly browned.
two Add the ginger, chilli and mushrooms
and sauté for 5 mins. Add the chilli powder,
turmeric, cumin, ground coriander, tomatoes
and sugar. Cover the saucepan and cook
gently for about 8–10 mins.
three Stir in the cream and fresh coriander,
season with salt and pepper and serve hot.

This is the perfect choice for
those who love aromatic rather
than fiery dishes.

oopma

preparation time **10 mins**
cooking time **20 mins**
total time **30 mins** serves **4**

175 g/6 oz coarse semolina
3 tablespoons vegetable oil
1 teaspoon black mustard seeds
1 teaspoon cumin seeds
1 dried red chilli, chopped
10–12 curry leaves
1 red onion, finely chopped
1 fresh green chilli, deseeded and
   chopped
50 g/2 oz raisins
2 tablespoons roasted cashew nuts
50 g/2 oz frozen peas
600 ml/1 pint hot water
1 tablespoon lemon juice
2 tablespoons freshly grated coconut,
   plus extra to serve
2 tablespoons chopped fresh coriander
sea salt and pepper
yogurt and cucumber, to serve

one Heat a large, heavy-based frying pan
over a medium heat and dry-fry the
semolina, stirring frequently, for 10 mins
or until it turns golden brown. Set aside.
two Heat the oil in a large, nonstick frying
pan and, when hot, add the mustard and
cumin seeds, dried chilli and curry leaves.
Stir-fry for 30 seconds, add the onion and
fresh chilli and stir-fry until the onion has
softened.
three Add the raisins, cashew nuts, peas,
semolina and water. Season and cook
gently, stirring, until the semolina has
absorbed all the water. Stir in the lemon
juice, coconut and coriander. Serve hot
with yogurt and cucumber, and grated
coconut.

Coarse semolina is used in this typical south Indian savoury
breakfast treat. Do not buy the fine semolina used for puddings
and sweets, or you will end up with a sticky mess. Coarse
semolina is widely available from Indian or Asian stores.
This would make a wonderful spicy Sunday brunch.

This cabbage dish uses urad dhal (a lentil), which
has a nutty flavour when it is fried or roasted.
It is used widely in many south Indian dishes.

cabbage bhaji

preparation time **10 mins**
cooking time **10 mins**
total time **20 mins** serves **4**

500 g/1 lb white cabbage, roughly chopped
150 ml/¼ pint water
1 tablespoon vegetable oil
2 teaspoons urad dhal
1 teaspoon black mustard seeds
1 dried red chilli, finely chopped
6–8 curry leaves
2 tablespoons grated fresh coconut
sea salt and pepper

one Put the cabbage into a large
saucepan with the water, cover and cook
over a medium heat for 10 mins, stirring
occasionally. Drain, return to the pan,
set aside and keep warm.
two Meanwhile, heat the oil in a small,
nonstick frying pan and, when hot, add the
urad dhal, mustard seeds and chilli. Stir-fry
for 1–2 mins and, when the dhal turns
light brown, add the curry leaves. Fry,
stirring constantly, for 2 mins.
three Pour this spiced oil over the
cabbage, stir in the coconut, season
with salt and pepper and serve hot.

jeera potatoes

preparation time **10 mins**
cooking time **10 mins**
total time **20 mins** serves **4**

2 tablespoons vegetable oil
1 tablespoon fresh root ginger,
    cut into fine slivers
1 tablespoon cumin seeds
500 g/1 lb potatoes, peeled, cut into
    2.5 cm/1 inch cubes and boiled
1 fresh green chilli, finely sliced
2 teaspoons lime juice
sea salt and pepper
fresh coriander leaves, to garnish

one Heat the oil in a large frying pan and,
when hot, add the ginger and cumin.
Stir-fry for 2 mins, then add the potatoes and
chilli. Season with salt and pepper and sauté
for 6–8 mins or until the potatoes
are lightly browned.
two Stir in the lime juice and sprinkle over
the coriander leaves. Serve hot.

Spiced with cumin, these potatoes
go well with chicken and fish dishes.

spinach and chickpea sabzi

preparation time **5 mins**
cooking time **20 mins**
total time **25 mins**   serves **4**

1 tablespoon vegetable oil
1 teaspoon cumin seeds
½ teaspoon coarsely ground coriander seeds
1 small onion, finely chopped
250 g/8 oz baby spinach
200 g/7 oz can chopped tomatoes
1 teaspoon chilli powder
1 tablespoon dhana-jeera (see page 9)
1 teaspoon amchur (dried mango powder)
1 teaspoon jaggery or soft brown sugar
1 tablespoon lime juice
400 g/13 oz can chickpeas, rinsed and drained
175 ml/6 fl oz water
sea salt and pepper

one Heat the oil in a large frying pan and, when hot, add the cumin and coriander seeds and onion. Stir-fry until the onion is soft and light brown, then add the spinach and tomatoes and stir well.

two Add the chilli powder, dhana-jeera, amchur, jaggery or sugar and lime juice and stir. Cook for 1–2 mins, then add the chickpeas and water. Season with salt and pepper, cover and simmer gently for 10 mins, stirring occasionally. Serve hot.

This quick, tasty dish uses spinach and canned chickpeas, flavoured with amchur (dried mango powder).

brinjal and potato curry

preparation time **10 mins**
cooking time **10–12 mins**
total time **20–22 mins** serves **4**

1 small onion, chopped
2 teaspoons grated fresh root ginger
5 garlic cloves, roughly chopped
2 fresh green chillies, deseeded and chopped
100 ml/3½ fl oz water
4 tablespoons vegetable oil
1 large aubergine, cut into 1 cm/
    ½ inch dice
500 g/1 lb potatoes, cut into 1 cm/
    ½ inch cubes, boiled and drained
2 teaspoons cumin seeds
1 teaspoon nigella
1 teaspoon ground turmeric
1 teaspoon ground coriander
1 teaspoon ground cumin
1 tablespoon lemon juice
sea salt and pepper
chopped fresh coriander leaves, to garnish

one Put the onion, ginger, garlic, chillies and water into a food processor or blender and process until smooth. Set aside.
two Heat 2 tablespoons of the oil in a large frying pan and, when hot, stir-fry the aubergine until lightly browned. Remove with a slotted spoon and set aside.
three Heat the remaining oil and, when hot, add the potatoes and cook until lightly browned. Remove with a slotted spoon and set aside.
four Add the cumin seeds and nigella to the pan, stir for 30 seconds, then add the turmeric, ground coriander, ground cumin and the onion paste. Fry for 2–3 mins, then return the potatoes and aubergines to the pan. Season with salt and pepper and stir-fry for 3–4 mins. Remove from the heat, stir in the lemon juice and serve hot, garnished with fresh coriander.

Aubergines ('brinjal') cooked with potatoes and spices are wonderful stuffed into a sandwich or served with rice and Tarka Dhal (see page 78).

bhindi bhaji

preparation time **10 mins**
cooking time **15 mins**
total time **25 mins** serves **4**

3 tablespoons vegetable oil
1 teaspoon mustard seeds
1 teaspoon cumin seeds
500 g/1 lb okra, trimmed and
    cut into 1 cm/½ inch slices
1 teaspoon chilli powder
1 tablespoon dhana-jeera (see page 9)
2 teaspoons jaggery or soft brown sugar
1 tomato, finely chopped
2 tablespoons chopped fresh coriander leaves
sea salt and pepper
lime wedges, to serve

one Heat the oil in a large frying pan and,
when hot, add the mustard and cumin seeds.
As soon as the mustard seeds begin to pop,
add the okra and stir-fry for 8–10 mins.
two Add the chilli powder, dhana-jeera,
jaggery or sugar and tomato and cook for
another 3–5 mins. Remove from the heat,
season with salt and pepper and stir in the
coriander. Serve hot with lime wedges,
to squeeze over.

Okra is cooked in various different
 ways in India. It can be stuffed
with a masala and fried, used in
curries or finely sliced and deep-
fried for a crunchy snack. Here it
is quickly stir-fried.

spiced beetroot

preparation time **10 mins**
cooking time **5–6 mins**
total time **15–16 mins** serves **4**

1 tablespoon vegetable oil
2 garlic cloves, finely chopped
1 teaspoon grated fresh root ginger
1 teaspoon cumin seeds
1 teaspoon coriander seeds, coarsely crushed
½ teaspoon dried red chilli flakes
625 g/1¼ lb freshly cooked and peeled
    beetroot, cut into wedges
150 ml/¼ pint coconut milk
¼ teaspoon ground cardamom seeds
grated rind and juice of 1 lime
handful of chopped fresh coriander leaves
sea salt and pepper

one Heat the oil in a large frying pan and,
when hot, add the garlic, ginger, cumin and
coriander seeds and chilli flakes. Stir-fry for
1–2 mins, then add the beetroot. Fry, stirring
gently, for 1 min, then add the coconut milk,
cardamom and lime rind and juice. Cook
over a medium heat for 2–3 mins.
two Stir in the fresh coriander, season with
salt and pepper and serve hot, warm or at
room temperature.

Gently spiced with cardamom, coriander, cumin and lime, this dish will change the way you feel about this colourful but humble root. Freshly cooked beetroot is now available everywhere; do not use those that have been preserved or cooked with vinegar.

Coconut milk perfectly complements the spiced pumpkin.

pumpkin curry

preparation time **10 mins**
cooking time **15–20 mins**
total time **25–30 mins** serves **4**

1 tablespoon vegetable oil
1 onion, halved and thinly sliced
4 garlic cloves, crushed
1 teaspoon ground cumin
2 teaspoons ground coriander
1 fresh green chilli, finely chopped
6 curry leaves
400 ml/14 fl oz can coconut milk
200 ml/7 fl oz hot water
750 g/1½ lb pumpkin, cut into
   5 cm/2 inch cubes
sea salt and pepper
2 tablespoons chopped fresh coriander leaves

one Heat the oil in a large saucepan and, when hot, add the onion. Stir-fry until soft and lightly browned. Add the garlic, cumin, ground coriander, chilli and curry leaves and stir-fry for another minute.
two Pour in the coconut milk, hot water and pumpkin and bring to the boil. Reduce the heat, cover and simmer gently for 10–15 mins or until the pumpkin is tender.
three Season with salt and pepper and stir in the fresh coriander. Serve hot.

mango curry

preparation time **10 mins**
cooking time **8–10 mins**
total time **18–20 mins** serves **4**

1 tablespoon vegetable oil
1 teaspoon mustard seeds
1 onion, halved and thinly sliced
15–20 curry leaves
½ teaspoon dried red chilli flakes
1 teaspoon grated fresh root ginger
1 fresh green chilli, deseeded and sliced
1 teaspoon ground turmeric
3 ripe mangoes, peeled, stoned and thinly
   sliced
400 ml/14 fl oz natural yogurt, lightly beaten
sea salt

one Heat the oil in a large saucepan and, when hot, add the mustard seeds, onion, curry leaves and chilli flakes. Fry, stirring, for 4–5 mins or until the onion is lightly browned.
two Add the ginger and fresh chilli to the onion mixture, stir-fry for 1 min, then add the turmeric. Stir to mix well, then remove the pan from the heat.
three Add the mangoes and yogurt and stir constantly until well mixed. Season to taste with salt. Return the pan to a low heat and heat through for 1 min, stirring constantly. (Do not let it boil or the curry will curdle.) Serve warm.

Use very ripe mangoes to ensure a really fruity flavour.

broccoli sabzi

preparation time **10 mins**
cooking time **15 mins**
total time **25 mins** serves **4**

2 tablespoons vegetable oil
1 teaspoon cumin seeds
1 onion, halved and finely sliced
1 fresh red chilli, finely sliced
3 garlic cloves, finely chopped
300 g/10 oz broccoli, cut into bite-sized florets
sea salt and pepper

one Heat the oil in a large, nonstick frying pan and, when hot, add the cumin. Stir-fry for 1 min, then add the onion. Cook over a medium heat until lightly browned.
two Stir in the chilli, garlic and broccoli. Cover the pan and reduce the heat to low. Cook for 6–8 mins or until the broccoli is just tender. Season with salt and pepper and serve hot.

This delicately spiced dish makes a good accompaniment to a heavily spiced curry.

shallot curry

preparation time **10 mins**
cooking time **18–20 mins**
total time **28–30 mins** serves **4**

2 tablespoons vegetable oil
1 teaspoon coarsely ground coriander seeds
1 teaspoon cumin seeds
3 plum tomatoes, roughly chopped
10 shallots, peeled
1 teaspoon chilli powder
½ teaspoon ground turmeric
1 tablespoon dhana-jeera (see page 9)
1 teaspoon sugar
4–6 tablespoons lemon juice
3 large potatoes, cut into matchsticks
150 ml/¼ pint water
2 tablespoons chopped fresh coriander leaves
sea salt and pepper

one Heat the oil in a large frying pan and, when hot, add the ground coriander, cumin seeds, tomatoes and shallots. Stir-fry for 2 mins, then add the chilli powder, turmeric, dhana-jeera, sugar and lemon juice to taste. Stir to mix well.

two Add the potatoes and water, cover and cook gently for 10–15 mins or until the potatoes are tender. Stir in the fresh coriander, season with salt and pepper and serve hot.

The delicate, sweet flavour of shallots is complemented
by the aromatic spices in this flavoursome curry.

rice and breads

Delicious, aromatic
and easy to make
kitchere, coconut
rice, naan bread and
spiced puris.

saffron and cardamom rice

preparation time **5 mins**,
   plus soaking and standing
cooking time **15 mins**
total time **20 mins** serves **4**

15 g/½ oz unsalted butter
1 tablespoon vegetable oil
1 onion, finely chopped
2 dried red chillies
6 cardamom pods, lightly crushed
1 cinnamon stick
1 teaspoon cumin seeds
2 bay leaves
225 g/7½ oz basmati rice, washed and
   soaked in cold water for 15 mins
1 teaspoon saffron threads, soaked
   in 1 tablespoon hot milk
475 ml/16 fl oz boiling water
sea salt and pepper
crispy fried onions, to garnish

one Heat the butter and oil in a large, heavy-based saucepan and add the onion. Stir and cook over a medium heat for 2–3 mins. Add the chillies, cardamom, cinnamon, cumin and bay leaves.

two Drain the rice, add to the pan and stir-fry for 2–3 mins. Add the saffron mixture and boiling water, season with salt and pepper and bring back to the boil. Cover tightly, reduce the heat to low and simmer gently for 10 mins. Do not lift the lid, as the steam is required for the cooking process.

three Remove the pan from the heat and leave the rice to stand, covered and undisturbed, for 8–10 mins. Fluff up the grains with a fork and serve garnished with crispy fried onions.

TIP To make crispy fried onions, thinly slice an onion and shallow-fry until crisp and golden. Drain on kitchen paper and serve sprinkled over rice dishes.

Flavoured with the aromatic spices cardamom and
saffron, this fragrant rice dish makes a delicious
centrepiece for any Indian meal.

This aromatic, delicately-flavoured and coloured rice would make a good dinner party dish.

tomato rice

preparation time **5 mins**,
    plus soaking and standing
cooking time **15 mins**
total time **20 mins** serves **4**

25 g/1 oz butter
1 small onion, halved and thinly sliced
1 garlic clove, crushed
1 teaspoon cumin seeds
4–6 black peppercorns
1 clove
1 cinnamon stick
225 g/7½ oz basmati rice, washed and soaked
    in cold water for 15 mins
50 g/2 oz frozen peas
200 g/7 oz can chopped tomatoes
2 tablespoons tomato purée
475 ml/16 fl oz boiling water
2 tablespoons chopped fresh coriander leaves
sea salt and pepper

one Heat the butter in a large, heavy-based saucepan and, when melted, add the onion, garlic, cumin, peppercorns, clove and cinnamon. Stir-fry for 2–3 mins. Drain the rice.

two Add the peas, tomatoes, tomato purée and rice and stir-fry for another 2–3 mins.

three Add the boiling water and coriander, season with salt and pepper and bring back to the boil. Cover tightly, reduce the heat to low and simmer gently for 10 mins. Do not lift the lid, as the steam is required for the cooking process.

four Remove the pan from the heat and leave the rice to stand, covered and undisturbed, for 8–10 mins. To serve, fluff up the grains of rice with a fork.

jeera rice

preparation time **5 mins**,
   plus soaking and standing
cooking time **15 mins**
total time **30 mins** serves **4**

25 g/1 oz unsalted butter
2 teaspoons cumin seeds
1 clove
2 cardamom pods, lightly crushed
225 g/7½ oz basmati rice, washed and soaked
   in cold water for 15 mins
475 ml/16 fl oz boiling water
sea salt and pepper

one Melt the butter in a large, heavy-based saucepan over a medium heat. Add the cumin, clove and cardamom and stir-fry for 30 seconds.

two Drain the rice, add to the pan and stir to coat in the spiced butter for 2–3 mins. Add the boiling water, season with salt and pepper and bring back to the boil. Cover tightly, reduce the heat to low and simmer for 10 mins. Do not lift the lid, as the steam is required for the cooking process.

three Remove the pan from the heat and leave the rice to stand, covered and undisturbed, for 8–10 mins. To serve, lightly fluff up the grains with a fork.

This simple rice dish, flavoured with cumin, makes a great accompaniment to any Indian meal.

kitchere

preparation time **5 mins**,
   plus soaking and standing
cooking time **18–20 mins**
total time **23–25 mins** serves **4**

15 g/½ oz unsalted butter
1 tablespoon vegetable oil
1 onion, halved and thinly sliced
1 cinnamon stick
4–5 cloves
6 black peppercorns
1 teaspoon grated fresh root ginger
2 fresh green chillies, deseeded and finely
   chopped
1 teaspoon cumin seeds
2 teaspoons ground coriander
100 g/3½ oz dried moong dhal (split yellow
   lentils), rinsed and drained
225 g/7½ oz basmati rice, rinsed and soaked in
   cold water for 15 mins
600 ml/1 pint boiling water
sea salt and pepper
crispy fried onions and hard-boiled eggs, to
   garnish

one Heat the butter and oil in a large, heavy-based saucepan and add the onion. Cook until lightly browned. Add the cinnamon, cloves, peppercorns, ginger, chillies, cumin, coriander, moong dhal and drained rice. Season and stir-fry for 3–4 mins.

two Add the water and bring back to the boil. Cover tightly, reduce the heat to low and cook for 10 mins. Do not lift the lid, as the steam is required for the cooking process. Remove from the heat and leave to stand, covered and undisturbed, for 8–10 mins.

three To serve, fluff up the grains of rice with a fork and garnish with crispy fried onions and hard-boiled eggs.

coconut rice

preparation time **5 mins**,
   plus soaking and standing
cooking time **15 mins**
total time **20 mins** serves **4**

2 tablespoons vegetable oil
2 teaspoons black mustard seeds
1 teaspoon cumin seeds
10 curry leaves
1 dried red chilli, finely chopped
225 g/7½ oz basmati rice, washed and soaked
   in cold water for 15 mins
100 ml/3½ fl oz coconut milk
375 ml/13 fl oz boiling water
sea salt and pepper
roasted cashew nuts, to garnish

one Heat the oil in a large, heavy-based saucepan and, when hot, add the mustard and cumin seeds, curry leaves and chilli.
two Drain the rice, add to the pan and stir-fry for 1–2 mins. Add the coconut milk and boiling water, season with salt and pepper and bring back to the boil. Cover tightly, reduce the heat to low and simmer gently for 10–12 mins. Do not lift the lid, as the steam is required for the cooking process.
three Remove the pan from the heat and leave to stand, covered and undisturbed, for 8–10 mins. To serve, fluff up the grains of rice with a fork and garnish with roasted cashew nuts.

Lightly spiced and fragrant with coconut milk, this
rice dish is the perfect partner for fish or seafood.

mushroom pulao

preparation time **10 mins**, plus standing
cooking time **18–20 mins**
total time **28–30 mins** serves **4**

25 g/1 oz unsalted butter
3–4 garlic cloves, thinly sliced
1 teaspoon grated fresh root ginger
3 spring onions, thinly sliced
½ teaspoon ground turmeric
250 g/8 oz chestnut mushrooms,
    thinly sliced
225 g/7½ oz easy-cook basmati rice, rinsed
    and drained
2 tablespoons chopped fresh coriander leaves
600 ml/1 pint boiling vegetable stock
    or water
sea salt and pepper

one Heat the butter in a large, heavy-based
saucepan and, when melted, add the
garlic, ginger, spring onions, turmeric,
mushrooms and rice. Stir-fry for 2–3 mins,
then add the coriander. Season with salt
and pepper, pour in the boiling stock or
water and bring back to the boil. Cover
tightly, reduce the heat to low and simmer
for 15 mins. Do not lift the lid, as the
steam is required for the cooking process.
two Remove the pan from the heat and
leave to stand, covered and undisturbed,
for 8–10 mins. To serve, fluff up the grains
of rice with a fork.

spinach and chickpea pulao

preparation time **5 mins**, plus standing
cooking time **15–18** mins
total time **20–23** mins serves **4**

15 g/½ oz unsalted butter
1 tablespoon vegetable oil
1 onion, finely chopped
1 teaspoon cumin seeds
2 teaspoons ground coriander
2 garlic cloves, crushed
1 teaspoon grated fresh root ginger
100 g/3½ oz spinach leaves, finely shredded
400 g/13 oz can chickpeas, rinsed and drained
225 g/7½ oz easy-cook basmati rice, rinsed
    and drained
2 tablespoons chopped dill
600 ml/1 pint boiling vegetable stock
sea salt and pepper

one Heat the butter and oil in a large,
heavy-based frying pan and, when hot,
add the onion. Cook over a medium heat
until lightly browned, then add the cumin,
coriander, garlic, ginger, spinach, chickpeas,
rice and dill. Stir and season with salt and
pepper.
two Pour over the boiling stock and bring
back to the boil. Cover tightly, reduce the
heat to low and cook gently for 10–12 mins.
Do not lift the lid, as the steam is required
for the cooking process.
three Remove the pan from the heat and
leave the rice to stand, covered and
undisturbed, for 8–10 mins. Fluff up the
grains with a fork and serve hot.

naan

preparation time **10 mins**, plus resting
cooking time **20 mins**
total time **30 mins** makes **8**

225 g/7½ oz self-raising flour, plus extra for
   dusting
5 g/¼ oz sachet fast-action dried yeast
1 teaspoon sea salt
1 teaspoon roasted cumin seeds
2 tablespoons natural yogurt, lightly beaten
1 tablespoon melted butter,
   plus extra for brushing
4 tablespoons lukewarm milk
vegetable oil, for oiling
fresh coriander leaves, to garnish

one In a large, warmed mixing bowl, mix
together the flour, yeast, salt, cumin,
yogurt and butter. Add the milk and knead
to make a soft dough. Cover with a lightly
oiled sheet of polythene and leave to rest
for 20–25 mins in a warm (not hot) place.
two Turn the dough out on to a large board
or surface lightly dusted with flour and
knead for 3–4 mins or until smooth. Divide
the dough into 8 portions and roll each one
up into a ball.
three With a rolling pin, roll each ball out
into an oval or triangular shape, the size of
a pitta bread.
four Brush with melted butter and cook in
batches under a preheated hot grill for 2–3
mins on each side. Serve hot, garnished
with coriander leaves.

VARIATION In place of the cumin seeds,
you can use 1 teaspoon nigella, poppy
seeds or sesame seeds. Alternatively, use
2 finely chopped garlic cloves.

Though readily available in
supermarkets and shops, there
is nothing like freshly made naan
bread. You can also vary the
flavourings used when you make
your own.

Quick and easy to prepare, these deep-fried puris (puffed up bread) are excellent served with Jeera Potatoes (see page 85), Brinjal and Potato Curry (see page 87) or Prawns with Curry Leaves and Fenugreek (see page 68).

spiced puris

preparation time **10 mins**
cooking time **20 mins**
total time **30 mins** makes **16**

225 g/7½ oz atta or chapatti flour
1 teaspoon hot chilli powder
1 teaspoon cumin seeds
½ teaspoon ground turmeric
1 teaspoon sea salt
1–2 tablespoons water
oil, for deep-frying

one Put the flour, chilli powder, cumin, turmeric and salt into a large mixing bowl and add enough water to make a soft but not sticky dough. Knead until the dough is smooth and elastic.

two Divide the dough into 16 portions and roll each one out to an 8 cm/3½ inch disc.

three Heat the oil in a large wok or deep frying pan to 180–190°C (350–375°F) or until a cube of bread browns in 30 seconds. Fry the puris in batches of 2–3. When the puris puff up, turn them over and fry until browned and crisp. Remove with a slotted spoon and drain on kitchen paper. Serve hot or at room temperature. They will keep for up to a week, if stored in an airtight container.

These puris make a quick and tasty snack. They are made with atta or chapatti flour, a medium-grade wheat flour which is sold in Indian and Asian shops.

bhaturas

preparation time **10 mins**, plus resting
cooking time **10 mins**
total time **20 mins** makes **10**

175 g/6 oz self-raising flour, plus extra for
  dusting
1 tablespoon oil
1 tablespoon natural yogurt
1 teaspoon sea salt
2–3 tablespoons water
oil, for deep-frying

one In a large mixing bowl, combine the flour, oil, yogurt and salt. Mix well and add enough water to make a soft dough. Cover with a tea towel and leave to rest for 15 mins.

two Turn the dough out on to a lightly floured board and knead well for 3–4 mins or until smooth. Divide the mixture into 10 portions and roll up each portion into a ball.

three Using a rolling pin, roll each ball into an 8 cm/3½ inch disc and set aside.

four Heat the oil for deep-frying in a large wok or deep frying pan to 180–190°C (350–375°F) or until a cube of bread browns in 30 seconds. Carefully slide 2–3 bhaturas into the pan. When the bhaturas puff up, turn them over and fry for 1 min or until lightly browned on both sides. Carefully remove with a slotted spoon and drain on kitchen paper. Repeat until all the bhaturas are fried and serve immediately.

desserts

Indian desserts are usually served on special religious and festive occasions. However, these gently flavoured and lightly spiced desserts are ideal for everyday cooking and entertaining.

shrikandh

preparation time **5 mins**, plus chilling (optional)
total time **5 mins** serves **4**

500 g/1 lb curd cheese
125 g/4 oz cream cheese
150 g/5 oz natural yogurt
3 tablespoons caster sugar
1 tablespoon rosewater
2 teaspoons crushed cardamom seeds
1 teaspoon saffron threads, soaked
   in 1 tablespoon hot water
finely chopped pistachio nuts and rose petals,
   to decorate

one In a large mixing bowl, beat together
the cheeses, yogurt, sugar, rosewater and
cardamom until smooth and glossy.
two Stir in the saffron mixture and mix
well. Cover and chill for a couple of hours,
if time allows.
three Sprinkle over chopped pistachio nuts
and rose petals before serving.

mango fool

preparation time **10 mins**, plus chilling
total time **10 mins** serves **4**

3 ripe mangoes, stoned and chopped
finely grated rind and juice of 1 lime
2 teaspoons soft brown sugar
250 ml/8 fl oz double cream, lightly whipped
diced mango, to decorate

one Put the mangoes, lime rind and juice
and sugar into a food processor or blender
and process until smooth. Transfer to a large
mixing bowl, fold in the whipped cream and
mix well.
two Pour the fool into 4 dessert glasses,
cover and chill for 3–4 hours until ready
to serve. Decorate with diced mango.

Always try to use the ripest
mangoes available.

This dessert, made with curd cheese and flavoured with
cardamom and saffron, was one of my childhood favourites.
It is really scrumptious when eaten with freshly made puris.

banana and cardamom pancakes

preparation time **10 mins**
cooking time **10–15 mins**
total time **20–25 mins** serves **4**

4 ripe bananas, mashed
300 g/10 oz self-raising flour
2 tablespoons caster sugar
2 tablespoons melted butter
100 ml/3½ fl oz milk
1 egg, lightly beaten
2 teaspoons crushed cardamom seeds
sunflower oil, for brushing

TO SERVE
vanilla ice cream
honey

one Put the bananas, flour, sugar, butter, milk and egg into a large mixing bowl and beat until smooth. Stir in the cardamom.
two Heat a large, nonstick frying pan and brush with oil. Pour in 3–4 tablespoonfuls of the batter and cook for 2–3 mins. Flip the pancakes over and cook for another 2 mins or until lightly browned and cooked through. Remove the pancakes with a slotted spoon and keep warm. Repeat with the remaining batter until all the pancakes are cooked.
three Serve 2–3 pancakes per person, with vanilla ice cream and honey.

Banana and cardamom are an unbeatable combination, so these pancakes are sure to become a family favourite.

coconut barfi

preparation time **10 mins**,
  plus chilling (optional)
cooking time **18–20 mins**
total time **28–30 mins** makes **12–15 squares**

4 tablespoons butter, plus extra for greasing
400 g/13 oz caster sugar
450 ml/¾ pint boiling water
250 g/8 oz grated fresh coconut
2 teaspoons crushed cardamom seeds
100 g/3½ oz pistachio nuts, roughly chopped,
  plus extra to decorate

This delicious coconut fudge is easy
to make and will keep in an airtight
container for up to one week, if it
hasn't all been eaten by then!

one Lightly grease a Swiss roll tin (about
30 x 20 cm/12 x 8 inches). Put the sugar into
a large, heavy-based saucepan with the
boiling water and bring back to the boil.
Cook over a medium heat for 8–10 mins or
until the syrup is reduced and thick.
two Stir in the butter, coconut and
cardamom and cook for another 10 mins,
stirring constantly. Remove from the heat
and stir in the pistachio nuts.
three Pour the mixture into the tin, spread
evenly and, when cool, chill for 6 hours, if
time allows. To serve, cut the barfi into
squares and garnish with extra chopped
pistachio nuts.

spiced caramelized pears with ginger cream

preparation time **10 mins**
cooking time **10–12 mins**
total time **20–22 mins** serves **4**

200 ml/7 fl oz double cream,
   lightly whipped
2 pieces stem ginger in syrup,
   finely chopped
1 tablespoon syrup from the jar
   of stem ginger

PEARS
2 tablespoons butter
4–5 firm dessert pears, peeled,
   cored and cut into thick slices
75 g/3 oz caster sugar
¼ teaspoon ground cinnamon
a pinch of ground cloves
½ teaspoon crushed cardamom seeds
100 g/3½ oz chopped walnuts

one Make the ginger cream by mixing together the cream, stem ginger and ginger syrup in a bowl. Cover and chill until ready to serve.

two Melt the butter in a large, nonstick frying pan and add the pears, sugar, cinnamon, cloves, cardamom and walnuts. Cook over a medium heat for 3–4 mins, stirring occasionally.

three Increase the heat to high and cook for 6–8 mins, stirring occasionally, until the pears are lightly caramelized. Serve hot, with tablespoonfuls of the ginger cream.

A sophisticated but easy dessert that is ideal for a dinner party.

gajjar halwa

preparation time **5 mins**
cooking time **25 mins**
total time **30 mins** serves **4**

750 ml/1¼ pints full-fat milk
300 g/10 oz carrots, roughly grated
40 g/1½ oz butter
1 tablespoon golden syrup
125 g/4 oz caster sugar
50 g/2 oz sultanas
1 teaspoon crushed cardamom seeds
finely flaked almonds, to decorate
vanilla ice cream or whipped cream,
    to serve

one Put the milk, carrots, butter, golden syrup, sugar, sultanas and cardamom into a large, heavy-based saucepan. Bring to the boil and cook over a medium heat for 20 mins, stirring frequently, until all the liquid has been absorbed and the mixture has thickened.
two Spread the halwa into a shallow dish and leave to stand until ready to serve.
three Sprinkle the flaked almonds over the halwa and serve with scoops of vanilla ice cream or whipped cream.

This rich and luscious dessert, made with carrots, is almost fudge-like in texture. Served warm with ice cream, who could ask for anything more?

seviyan

preparation time **5 mins**
cooking time **15 mins**
total time **20 mins** serves **4**

25 g/1 oz butter
100 g/3½ oz dried vermicelli
400 ml/14 fl oz milk
200 ml/7 fl oz water
pinch of saffron threads
150 g/5 oz caster sugar
50 g/2 oz toasted flaked almonds
½ teaspoon crushed cardamom seeds

one Heat the butter in a large saucepan and, when melted, add the vermicelli, breaking it into smaller pieces. Fry, stirring, until the vermicelli turns light brown.
two Pour the milk and water into the saucepan with the saffron. Mix well and bring to the boil. Continue to boil for 8–10 mins, then add the sugar. Reduce the heat to medium, cover the pan and cook until the vermicelli is tender and most of the liquid has been absorbed.
three Stir in the almonds and cardamom and serve hot or chilled.

This traditional dessert is made with vermicelli. Use the vermicelli found in Asian greengrocers, as it is a finer variety.

These sweet samosas are delicious hot, straight from the oven. Serve with lightly whipped cream or ice cream.

chocolate and banana samosas

preparation time **15 mins**
cooking time **15 mins**
total time **30 mins** makes **12**

2 ripe bananas, roughly mashed
1 tablespoon dark chocolate chips
12 filo pastry sheets, each about
    30 x 18 cm (12 x 7 inches)
melted butter, for brushing
icing sugar, for dusting

one Line a baking sheet with baking paper. Mix the banana with the chocolate chips and set aside.

two Fold each sheet of filo pastry in half lengthways. Place a large spoonful of the banana mixture at one end of the filo strip and then fold the corner of the filo over the mixture, covering it in a triangular shape. Continue folding the pastry over along the length of the pastry strip to make a neat triangular samosa. Moisten the edge with water to seal and place on the baking sheet. Repeat with the remaining filling and pastry.

three Brush the samosas with melted butter and bake in a preheated oven, 180°C (350°F), Gas Mark 4, for 12–15 mins or until lightly golden and crisp. Remove from the oven, dust with icing sugar and serve hot.

TIP When working with filo pastry, always keep the pastry covered with a damp tea towel to prevent it from drying out, until ready to use.

kheer

preparation time **5 mins**, plus chilling (optional)
cooking time **25 mins**
total time **30 mins** serves **4**

100 g/3½ oz Thai jasmine rice
750 ml/1¼ pints full-fat milk
3 tablespoons caster sugar
½ teaspoon grated nutmeg
1 teaspoon crushed cardamom seeds
50 g/2 oz pistachio nuts, chopped,
    plus extra to garnish
varq (silver leaf), to garnish (optional)

one Put the rice, milk and sugar into a large, heavy-based saucepan and bring to the boil. Reduce the heat and simmer for 10 mins. Add the nutmeg, cardamom and pistachio nuts and continue to cook for another 10 mins, stirring frequently, until the mixture is thick and creamy.

two Pour into 4 serving bowls, cover and chill for at least 6 hours before serving, if time allows. Garnish with pistachio nuts and varq, if liked.

This Indian version of rice pudding is delicately flavoured with nutmeg, cardamom and pistachio nuts. I use Thai jasmine rice, which results in a creamier texture. Serve chilled.

drinks and coolers

Tropical and exotic
fruits and spices
such as mango,
watermelon,
lemongrass and
cardamom flavour
these delicious hot
and cold beverages.

mango lassi

preparation time **10 mins**
total time **10 mins** serves **4**

3 fresh ripe mangoes, peeled, stoned
    and roughly chopped, or 300 ml/½ pint
    canned mango pulp
500 ml/17 fl oz natural yogurt
250 ml/8 fl oz water
1–2 tablespoons caster sugar

one Put the fresh mango, if using, into a
food processor or blender and blend until
smooth. Set aside.
two Blend the yogurt, water and sugar until
smooth. Divide the mango pulp between
4 tall glasses and pour over the yogurt
mixture. Serve chilled.

banana lassi

preparation time **10 mins**
total time **10 mins** serves **4**

3 ripe bananas, roughly chopped
500 ml/17 fl oz natural yogurt
250 ml/8 fl oz cold water
1–2 tablespoons caster sugar
¼ teaspoon ground cardamom seeds

one Put all the ingredients into a food
processor or blender and blend until
smooth. Pour into tall glasses and
serve chilled.

This makes an ideal
breakfast drink.

A version of this chilled, saffron-flavoured milkshake is usually made on festive occasions.

kesar cooler

preparation time **10 mins**
total time **10 mins** serves **4**

1 tablespoon ground almonds
1 teaspoon saffron threads
1 tablespoon chopped pistachio nuts,
    plus extra to decorate
½ teaspoon crushed cardamom pods
2 tablespoons caster sugar
3 tablespoons hot water
1 litre/1¾ pints cold milk
2–3 scoops vanilla ice cream

one Put the almonds, saffron, pistachio nuts, cardamom and sugar into a mortar, add the hot water and, using a pestle, grind well to make a paste.
two Transfer the paste to a food processor or blender and add the milk and ice cream. Blend well until smooth.
three Pour into chilled glasses and serve, decorated with chopped pistachio nuts.

watermelon cooler

preparation time **10 mins**,
    plus chilling (optional)
total time **10 mins** serves **4–6**

1 large, ripe watermelon
pinch of salt
a few mint leaves, to decorate

one Peel and deseed the watermelon, then cut into cubes. Put into a food processor or blender (you might have to do this in 2 batches) and blend until fairly smooth. Transfer to a large jug and add a pinch of salt. Stir to mix well and chill, covered, for 3–4 hours before serving.
two Serve in tall glasses, decorated with mint leaves.

mango and mint sherbet

preparation time **5 mins**
total time **5 mins** serves **4**

3 ripe mangoes, peeled, stoned and roughly
    chopped
4 tablespoons lemon juice
1 tablespoon caster sugar
12 mint leaves, finely chopped
900 ml/1½ pints ice cold water
ice cubes

one Put the mango, lemon juice, sugar
and mint leaves into a food processor or
blender with the water and blend until
smooth. To serve, pour into ice-filled
glasses.

This milky tea, lightly spiced with
ginger, cardamom, cloves and
cinnamon, is drunk all over India.

masala chai

preparation time **10 mins**
cooking time **10 mins**
total time **20 mins** serves **4**

6 teaspoons Darjeeling tea leaves
200 ml/7 fl oz milk
¼ teaspoon ground ginger
¼ teaspoon crushed cardamom seeds
⅛ teaspoon ground cloves
1 cinnamon stick
1 tablespoon caster sugar
900 ml/1½ pints water

one Put all the ingredients into a large
saucepan and bring to a rolling boil.
Reduce the heat to low and simmer for
5–6 mins. Strain into 4 large mugs or
glasses. Serve hot.

limboo soda

preparation time **10 mins**
total time **10 mins** serves **4**

juice of 6 limes
3 tablespoons caster sugar
10 mint leaves
1 litre/1¾ pints ice cold soda water
crushed ice and lime slices, to serve

one In a small bowl, stir together the lime
juice, sugar and mint leaves until the sugar
has dissolved.
two Pour into a large jug or pitcher and add
the soda water. Stir to mix well and pour
into 4 tall glasses filled with crushed ice and
lime slices.

lemongrass tea

preparation time **5 mins**
cooking time **5–7 mins**
total time **10–12 mins** serves **4**

3–4 lemongrass stalks, finely chopped
4 teaspoons Indian tea leaves
   (Darjeeling or Assam)
900 ml/1½ pints water

TO SERVE
milk
sugar

one Put the lemon grass and tea leaves into
a large saucepan with the water and bring to
the boil. Reduce the heat and simmer,
uncovered, for 2–3 mins. Strain and serve
hot, adding milk and sugar to taste.

cardamom coffee

preparation time **5 mins**
cooking time **5–7 mins**
total time **10–12 mins** serves **4**

3 tablespoons strong freshly ground coffee
   (South Indian, Colombian
   or Javan)
1 teaspoon crushed cardamom seeds
300 ml/½ pint milk
2 tablespoons caster sugar
750 ml/1¼ pints water

one Put the coffee, cardamom, milk, sugar
and water into a large saucepan and bring
to the boil. Reduce the heat and simmer
for 12 mins. Using a very fine sieve lined
with muslin, strain into a jug. Pour into
glasses or mugs and serve hot.

Limboo soda (left) also makes a terrific aperitif
with a generous slug of vodka, while the kesar
cooler (see page 122) is wonderfully refreshing.

Index

Acknowledgements

Executive Editor: Sarah Ford
Project Editor: Jessica Cowie
Executive Art Editor: Geoff Fennell
Designer: Sue Michniewicz

Photographer: William Reavell
Stylist: Liz Hippisley
Home Economist: Sunil Vijayakar
Production Controller: Ian Paton